# Developing Play for the Under 3s

The Treasure Basket and Heuristic Play approach is astoundingly simple – offering natural and household objects to babies and toddlers can have a profound impact on their learning capabilities, encouraging concentration, exploration and intellectual development.

Based on a wealth of research into how babies learn, *Developing Play for the Under 3s* shows how the use of this approach can transform the learning abilities of babies and toddlers. Featuring never before published, original interviews with the pioneer of the Treasure Basket and Heuristic Play, Elinor Goldschmied, this second edition includes:

- accessible explanations of what babies think and do;
- links to child development and learning progress;
- a new chapter on supporting the learning of two- and three-year-olds;
- links to the Early Years Foundation Stage outcomes;
- research evidence supported by case studies;
- resource ideas and activities for use in the nursery or at home.

Anita M. Hughes uses her own personal experience of working with the under 3s to guide readers through the benefits of the Treasure Basket and Heuristic Play. Providing clear and practical guidelines, this book is indispensible for anyone involved in the care of children in this age group who wishes to create rich learning experiences.

**Anita M. Hughes** is an independent chartered educational psychologist and has been working in the field of Early Years for the past 28 years.

# Developing Play for the Under 3s

## The Treasure Basket and Heuristic Play

## Second edition

Anita M. Hughes

**Routledge**
Taylor & Francis Group

LONDON AND NEW YORK

First edition published 2006
by David Fulton Publishers

This edition published 2010
by Routledge
2 Park Square, Milton Park, Abingdon, Oxon, OX14 4RN

Simultaneously published in the USA and Canada
by Routledge
270 Madison Avenue, New York, NY 10016

*Routledge is an imprint of the Taylor & Francis Group, an informa business*

© 2010 Anita M. Hughes

Typeset in Bembo and Frutiger by Book Now Ltd, London
Printed and bound in Great Britain by TJ International Ltd, Padstow,
Cornwall

*British Library Cataloguing in Publication Data*
A catalogue record for this book is available from the British Library

*Library of Congress Cataloging-in-Publication Data*
Hughes, Anita M.
Developing play for the under 3s: the Treasure Basket and Heuristic Play /
Anita M. Hughes.—2nd ed.
    p. cm.
Includes bibliographical references and index.
1. Learning by discovery. 2. Early childhood education. 3. Children—Study
and teaching (Early childhood) I. Title.
LB1067.H84 2010
155.42′28—dc22                                          2009040672

ISBN10: 0–415–56122–1 (hbk)
ISBN10: 0–415–56121–3 (pbk)
ISBN10: 0–203–85442–X (ebk)

ISBN13: 978–0–415–56122–8 (hbk)
ISBN13: 978–0–415–56121–1 (pbk)
ISBN13: 978–0–203–85442–6 (ebk)

*For Peter and Angela*

# Contents

List of figures                                                          ix

Foreword to the first edition                                            xi

Preface to the second edition                                           xiii

Acknowledgements                                                         xv

Introduction                                                              1

1  A tribute to Elinor Goldschmied                                        5

2  How babies and children learn                                         13

3  The beginning of sensory and physical development                     27

4  The Treasure Basket: 'What is the object like?'                       33

5  Offering the Treasure Basket                                          47

6  Heuristic Play: 'What can I do with the object?'                      61

7  Offering Heuristic Play material                                      75

8  Play with a purpose (two- to three-year-olds):
   'What can this object become?'                                        87

9  Expanding the approach                                                95

10 Conclusion                                                           105

References and further reading                                          107

# Figures

4.1 Babies around a Treasure Basket are totally absorbed as they examine, handle, mouth and shake the different objects 42

5.1 The Treasure Basket contains 80–100 different household and natural objects, which are safe but small enough for a baby to pick up and handle 48

5.2 Collect objects of different colour, texture, taste, smell, weight and temperature. They can be made of metal, wood, leather, rubber, raffia and bristle, as well as natural objects 50

5.3 The attentive caregiver provides an atmosphere of safety and trust so the baby feels confident to explore the objects in the Treasure Basket 58

6.1 Heuristic Play: a time of activity, purpose and intense concentration 66

7.1 The objects are attractively set out at the beginning of a Heuristic Play session 81

7.2 The caregiver is gentle and responsive towards the toddler's show of curiosity and interest during a Heuristic Play session 83

8.1 Using objects from our real world enhances make-believe play and promotes language development 89

## Figures

8.2 The role-play area allows the young child to copy
routine and domestic behaviours observed in adults          91

9.1 In the third year of life children begin to play together
and use their imagination. Here a box and tubes have
become a boat and mast                                       99

# Foreword to the first edition

I am thankful that it is Anita, who has at last written this book with such integrity and clarity. Over the years, we have had many conversations about the subject. I have enjoyed the 'tick tack tock', the briskness of our rapport, the interchange of our ideas and the words used to express those ideas.

What I like so much is seeing the rattle of our ideas taking form in her words and pictures. I like the word 'rattle' because it creates the image that there is a lot of content floating about, which is graspable, measurable, describable, definable and enjoyable. As we have battled on and managed to reach a definition of things, Anita has been able to expand and explain these ideas with clarity and polish.

I like the lively imagery that Anita uses through her case studies, which can take people away from the banal and give a fresh look to the scene. When I think about Anita, the image of bunches of flowers comes to mind, which seems to be very simple, but in fact is quite sophisticated. I hope that the quality of Anita's content will be appreciated and be sufficient to stand up to inspection and assessment. I feel enormous trust, because it is not an easy thing to do, to be able to clarify and expand these ideas with the attention to detail which Anita has shown.

This book will provide the opportunity for a new depth of understanding of the Treasure Basket and Heuristic Play. I hope it will stimulate further thought about current ideas, prejudices, confusions and inadequacies.

Elinor Goldschmied
October 2005

# Preface to the second edition

Since the publication of the first edition of my book, there has been the introduction of the Early Years Foundation Stage (EYFS) in England. This is a central part of the childcare strategy 'Choice for Parents, the Best Start for Children' and the Childcare Act (2006). It provides a coherent and flexible approach to care and learning for children from birth to five years. Alongside the *Statutory Framework for the Early Years Foundation Stage*, the department for Education and Skills (DfES 2007a) has provided the *Practice Guidance for the Early Years Foundation Stage* (DfES 2007b). This document provides practitioners with information and advice within each of the six areas covered by early learning goals. The six areas are:

1. Personal, Social and Emotional Development (PSED)
2. Communication, Language and Literacy (CLL)
3. Problem Solving, Reasoning and Numeracy (PSRN)
4. Knowledge and Understanding of the World (KUW)
5. Physical Development (PD)
6. Creative Development (CD).

The EYFS has deliberately divided up children's development into different areas as a way of categorising children's learning to help Early Years practitioners focus their attention and make sense of it. However, children's play does not fall into neat categories. Play, by its very nature of being creative and precarious, goes beyond the limits of intellectual categorisation. Indeed, when a child's play is observed it is likely that several of the identified areas of the EYFS are being covered at once. In my recent book

(2009), I provided practical guidance to support practitioners and students in the area that focuses on PRSN, but found there were cross-links all over the place!

In this new edition of *Developing Play for the Under 3s*, I will make links to the EYFS framework and show how the Treasure Basket and Heuristic Play experiences link to all developmental areas (see Chapters 4, 6 and 9). I have also added a new chapter, which focuses specifically on the play of two- to three-year-olds, as many readers have asked how the principles of Heuristic Play develop once children begin to use language. Throughout the book, I urge the reader to pay attention to my comments about the role of the adult. I often refer to the need to be responsive and attentive, but this also means being unobtrusive. In our enthusiasm to offer babies and children encouragement and to be 'seen as doing something', caregivers regularly fall into the trap of being unwittingly intrusive and interfering, thus hindering children's natural development and creativity.

Since writing the first edition of this book, my dear friend and colleague Elinor Goldschmied has died in February 2009 at the age of 98. I have therefore decided to include a tribute to her life and work in a whole new chapter, which will give readers the chance to gain some insight into how the concept of the Treasure Basket for babies came into being over 60 years ago.

This book is about very young children and their play and will interest grandparents, parents, Early Years practitioners and students. My passion for babies and children began when I worked in day nurseries, but my understanding came from becoming a mother and watching my own children. Although there is specific guidance for those working in group settings, it is my hope that this book will excite families and professionals alike.

# Acknowledgements

Without the wisdom, encouragement and friendship of Elinor Goldschmied this book would never have been written. She was the source of inspiration that gave birth to the Treasure Basket 60 years ago and Heuristic Play 25 years ago. I am deeply grateful for all her support during our 25-year working friendship and, in particular, throughout the writing of this book. She helped me to retain clarity of thought and to pay attention to detail throughout.

I would also like to thank Gwen Macmichael, my friend and colleague, who was with me from the start, as we embraced these ideas together, for her constant faith that I would be able to express this approach with compassion and integrity.

I would also like to express my appreciation of Katrin Stroh and Thelma Robinson, for their dynamic and innovative ideas on Functional Learning, which have helped me to gain a deeper understanding of how children learn with Heuristic Play materials.

To my other friends and colleagues, who not only supported me through my times of doubt as well as enthusiasm but also encouraged me to see the project through, I would like to express my heartfelt gratitude. They are Diane Sylvester, Dereca Trevail, Tess Tatham, Jeanette Walker, Heather Geddes, Barbara Robinson, Kim Yorkshire and Gemini Jones (of Nature Play) and my friends from the SDF course at Surrey University.

There are also the countless other wonderful people whom I would like to thank, who over the years have attended my workshops and expressed enthusiasm about this approach. Without their urgings, I might never have had the confidence to write for a wider audience.

Thanks, too, must go to my patient and responsive publishing editor, Margaret Marriott, who metaphorically took me by the hand, saying she believed I could create this book, and then sent me off to do it. Her prompt feedback and attention to detail at every step of the way have helped me to see the project to completion.

I would like to thank the staff and parents from Maxilla Nursery (London) and Asquith Nursery (Kingston) for kindly letting me take photos of the babies and young children in their care. I would also like to thank Nature Play (Surrey) and Haven Children's Centre (Hampshire) for providing me with such wonderful photos of children in their case.

It is hard to put into words the depth of gratitude I feel towards my husband, Graham, who has lived through my ups and downs during this long process, always being there for me. Probably the greatest thanks of all go to my children, Peter and Angela (now grown up) who have taught me (from babyhood) more than anyone else about the ideas I have shared in this book.

Finally, I would like to thank those of you who read this book and make these approaches part of your practice, so enriching the lives of babies and young children fortunate enough to come into your care.

# Introduction

It was during the very early 1980s, when Gwen Macmichael and I worked with Elinor Goldschmied, that we all gave the name 'Heuristic Play' to the exploratory play of toddlers. It was intended to help us make sense of the perplexing activity of very young children in nursery day care, as they played listlessly with 'table top' toys. Often, these toys were thrown about or hidden around the playroom.

As we unravelled, together with the nursery staff, what the children were actually doing, clear purposeful exploration and sophisticated learning became apparent. The more we varied the material, and offered open-ended natural and household objects and containers (rather than the inset puzzles, shape sorters, stacking boxes and rings, etc.), the more the children played purposefully, with calm and deep concentration. This fascinated us.

Over the past 20 or so years, through Elinor's unstinting teaching, writing and film making (together with my own humble contribution), the name 'Heuristic Play' has found its way into the language of early child development. What was at first seen as an eccentric way of looking at things, has now become valued as an essential element in understanding the way in which very young children use objects to develop conceptual thinking, just before the onset of expressive language.

However, although the term 'Heuristic Play' is becoming part of everyday parlance, many people do not know what it means. It is often referred to as 'holistic play'. It is also confused and interchanged with the term 'Treasure Basket'. It is my hope that this book will clarify these uncertainties and excite you, the reader, to re-examine what you give babies and toddlers to play with and *how* you respond to them in their play. Furthermore, I would like you to think about your own understanding of how babies and very young children learn.

Take time to observe babies and toddlers yourself. Notice how you respond to them and how intrusive, or not, you are when they play. Ask yourself whether or not you agree with the ideas put forward. Is there an even greater depth to the learning than I have described? What kind of subtle interaction is taking place between adults and children? What interaction really takes place between children under the age of three? Are children really calmer and more engaged when they play with natural and household materials rather than manufactured plastic toys? These questions need to be asked because our understanding of this play is only in its infancy.

## The three stages of play with objects

The way in which babies and very young children play with objects goes through three stages, which are very clear and distinct. However, when new material is introduced, a toddler or older child may revert to mouthing it before more sophisticated exploration or imaginative play takes place.

Approximately 5–10 months

- When a seated baby at the mouthing stage is offered an object to play with, the predominant interest is: 'What is this object like?'

Approximately 10–20 months

- When the baby becomes mobile and is able to explore how he can make objects interact with his environment, the predominant interest is: 'What can I do with it?' and 'What else can I do with it?'

From approximately 20 months onwards

- As the child begins to develop the use of language and he begins to understand the function of objects, the predominant interest is: 'What can this object become?'

## What is the Treasure Basket?

The Treasure Basket is a unique approach, which was pioneered and developed by Elinor Goldschmied (Goldschmied and Jackson 1994). In this approach the adult offers a seated baby (who cannot yet move independently) a range of natural, household and recycled objects, contained in a rigid, low-sided round basket, for exploration and interest. It is a deceptively simple idea, but these objects form the initial gateway to independent contact with the outside world and create the first opportunity for making choices and decisions. This is the developmental stage in infancy where the predominant interest is to handle and mouth objects in order to find out about their physical characteristics. If a baby had language, his main question would be: 'What is this object like?'

> We can never truly know what it is like to bite into a ripe juicy peach until we have actually taken a bite for ourselves. Similarly, what do the concepts cool and smooth, prickly and rough actually mean unless we have caressed a pebble, picked up a pine cone or fingered the bark of a gnarled tree?
> (Quote from conversation with Elinor Goldschmied in 1990)

The objects in a Treasure Basket can be described as 'food for the brain' as every new sensory experience makes the brain grow and become more active. The greater the variety of objects, the greater the mental stimulation and satisfaction for the baby. However, the value of the objects will only be realised if the caregiver is sitting comfortably nearby, attentive and responsive to the baby's needs, interest and safety.

## What is Heuristic Play?

The term 'Heuristic Play' is used to describe the activity of a toddler when he plays with *objects*. This term was first used by Elinor Goldschmied (Goldschmied and Jackson 1994) following collaborative work with Gwen Macmichael (play consultant and teacher) and myself in the early 1980s.

This play is not a social activity as it concerns how the toddler experiments with objects and the environment. However, toddlers will naturally pay attention to each other and may copy or interact with each other at times. It is also important that the attentive adult is always seated comfortably nearby to provide reassurance, a sense of safety and to share in the pleasure and amusement. In addition, it is the adult's role to provide the right kind of materials and the calm space to facilitate this play.

This play can be described as 'experimental', as the toddler's primary interest is to discover what he can do with the objects he finds. This is the next stage on from the primary interest of the seated baby who, through mouthing, wants to discover what the objects are like (their physical characteristics as experienced through the senses). Heuristic Play is, however, more than a typical set of actions with objects, it is a natural and creative way of living and is the basis on which all future problem-solving, scientific and mathematical learning will take place. Indeed, all activity which involves experimenting with how material can be manipulated can be described as heuristic. It starts in toddlerhood but is carried on throughout childhood and into adult life.

## Some thoughts about plastic

It will become apparent as you read the book, that my views on plastic toys appear negative. Indeed, my first publishing editor commented, 'Your points throughout the book come across as a personal plastic vendetta'. I do not want to appear set against anything. However, the torrent of manufactured plastic toys, which has increasingly smothered babies and young children over the past 50 years, is of great concern to me. Rather than plastic adding to a young child's experience, it seems to be largely replacing all other materials in a young child's life. This is especially so for a child living in an urban environment with little access to nature.

Rather than wanting to appear negative, it is my wish to open your eyes to the 'wonders of ordinariness' (natural and household material) and the 'limitations of technology' (sophisticated plastic toys) from a very young child's point of view.

## The use of the terms 'he' and 'she'

When writing this book, I decided to make a clear distinction between the terms 'he' and 'she', so there would be no confusion. The term 'she' refers to the caregiver and the term 'he' refers to the baby or child. This is not to assume that women are the only caregivers. Indeed, it delights me that we are in an era of increasingly shared parental care and rising numbers of male Early Years practitioners. I also hope that you will accept the term 'he' to refer to any male or female child. In my experience of observing babies and children in the very early years, any gender differences in their play are barely apparent.

# CHAPTER 1

# A tribute to Elinor Goldschmied

Elinor Goldschmied died on 27 February 2009 at the age of 98. Since her death, she has been heralded as a 'great thinker' and a 'pioneering expert' of the twentieth century. While this is undoubtedly true, she would be personally horrified by such adulation, as she was one of the humblest people I have ever met and was never interested in personal recognition. All Elinor ever wanted was to have her ideas understood and put into practice. Indeed, her ideas were incredibly practical and simple and she always paid particular attention to detail. Her favourite quotation, from William Blake, was, 'He who would do good to others must do it in minute particulars'. Elinor devoted her entire adult life towards improving professional practice in the care and well-being of babies and young children.

Her three main contributions were:

1.  the Treasure Basket
2.  Heuristic Play
3.  the Key Person approach.

In 2001 and 2002, I recorded several conversations that Elinor and I had together, and I have decided to include some extracts in this edition to give readers some background information on how her ideas came into being. One day, I asked Elinor what she thought was her most important idea and, without hesitation, she answered 'the Treasure Basket'.

I then probed into how she got the idea in the first place and this led on to her telling me pieces of her life story. We are all influenced by our earliest experiences and they shape our thinking and our attitudes for the rest of our lives. Elinor was born in 1910 into a prosperous family in rural Gloucestershire. She was the middle child of seven children and was educated at home during her early years. However, her idyllic life was shattered when, at the age of eight, her favourite eldest brother died and then, soon after, her mother died too.

Elinor's roots are in the natural world; a place of freedom and discovery. I shall now tell you something about Elinor's early life in her own words.

*Anita:* You always talk about the importance of minute particulars. Where do you think this came from?

*Elinor:* I think my way of thinking comes from looking at the minutiae. Did I ever tell you about lying on the grass when I was a little girl? Well, it was a garden lawn and I measured out a little space about as big as a handkerchief. I was giving strictly focused attention on what existed on a 'piece of a surface of the earth'! Lying on my stomach, I thought, 'I'm going to trawl every tiny visual variety, tactile variety, smell variety and temperature variety which I can observe in that space'. I might see a thing like an earwig, which was enormous compared to the grass strand, struggling to climb over that piece of grass. And getting down to the actual size of what that piece of grass was – and gearing oneself into the earwig's world and seeing what the challenge for the earwig was because everything was huge.

Somehow I was tackling this business of space and presence in space and how much was it possible to visualise oneself in a space which was enormous and yet there it was, covered by my hand. It's the same as the fascination I had with the story *Gulliver's Travels*. I always had a lovely illustrated copy of *Gulliver's Travels*. This business of being tiny and large (like the story of Alice in Wonderland) had a real resonance in my childhood, partly because it was my real experience. I had a very tall uncle and I remember his large feet that were like a picture of the enormous Gulliver's feet. I felt like the tiny Gulliver. I saw the adults in 'layers' somehow.

*Anita:* Tell me something about the Treasure Basket and why you think it is so important?

*Elinor:* The Treasure Basket is an attitude of mind; an attitude of observation. The way I use to formulate it is, 'everything is there and the only limitation is me!' I am in the world now, here. What I am able to select from, or separate out or focus on is entirely up to me. Therefore the Treasure Basket provides a whole world in focused form because it is deliberately collected to embrace a part of what is there.

*Anita:* How did you conceptualise the idea of the Treasure Basket in the first place?

*Elinor:* I would think through my early childhood experiences in the countryside. We had no toys but we would have something like a trowel, something you could dig with and acres of time playing in and around a stream that ran through our orchard. The stream was full of stones and interesting shells. There must have been some geological movements at some period because there were an awful lot of stones and shells of different kinds. We spent hours of time playing with mud, water, leaves; all the natural things. Every single thing became an element of interest.

When I think back to childhood and what we did in the countryside it was terribly dangerous but you did not fall out of a tree! And you did the balancing thing and the water was down there but somehow you knew very well what you could do and couldn't do.

We had tea parties too, made up of berries and stems and bits of shells ... really the collection. So the collection, which is really the Treasure Basket had in it all these natural elements, which were enormously varied, of course, given enough time and space.

We know those experiences are not accessible to the urban child or the rural child either, these days, because of pesticides and what not. So the availability of instruments for exploration and imagination is not easily there. I imagine that what we are doing is finding alternatives to be available. Mostly the alternatives are plastic toys. A load of oddments as in the Treasure Basket is never thought of as educational material. The Treasure Basket is a very sophisticated concept, but it is also unconventional. It is blindingly simple but appears difficult for most people to do. I wonder what it is that trips people up and why they don't 'get it'? The objects are eminently chooseable. They aren't too sophisticated.

There should be no such thing as a toy, really. They have no basic reality; they are invented. It's only real because it has a function invented by someone else to do something. Some elaborate toys have only one function and you can't combine them in different ways; you have to put it together or play with it 'that way'. A pile of plastic is a desolate sight; there is brittleness about it. It can't be mended. There are some good toys that give a variety of options like Lego, but there are not many.

*Anita:* Tell me something about your professional career and how you became so interested in the education, mental health and care of very young children.

*Elinor:* It started when I trained as a nursery teacher at the Froebel Institute in Roehampton, Surrey. It was a way of getting away from home and it was very good indeed. My first job was in the junior school of Dartington Hall in Devon and I was there for five years during the 1930s. I met up with some interesting people, who were in the theatre and so on and then I became politically interested. Very early on I took myself to the Soviet Union. I think I was about 21 or 22. I just signed myself up for one of these tours ... there were these tours to the Soviet Union. A couple of the theatre directors signed up for the Society for Cultural Relations with the USSR. A friend was one of the secretaries of the society, so she organised for me to go. It was £28 for 28 days. You just arrived at Victoria station in London and then we went by train from Ostende to Lubke. I was rather good at doing that kind of thing! Then on that kind of trip you met people and made connections.

Another thing that influenced me was my stepmother. She went into a menopausal depression and became quite mad. She spent 14 years in a mental institution. It wasn't understood in those days and I followed her suffering with terrible pain because she suffered. She was an intelligent woman and she realised what was happening and my poor father couldn't make head nor tail of it. She was at home a lot of the time looking like a ghost; it was a very severe depression. In a way I was caring for her indirectly and that directed me really towards mental health training. I wasn't frightened by my stepmother's mental disorder. In 1937, I was lucky enough to get a scholarship to the mental health course at the LSE [London School of Economics] to train as a psychiatric social worker. It was there I met my late husband Guido, who was Jewish and had been driven from his home town of Trieste by the fascist regime.

During the war I found myself running 'playgroups' for evacuated parents and their children. I put it together with anything I could find because there was no play material to be bought in the war. In a way the terrain was perfect because you couldn't buy anything so the obvious thing was to use what you could. No one had any difficulties about accepting that because there wasn't anything else. I didn't have to do any campaigning about that. The local authorities had to provide something for these East End mothers who were always complaining and pining for their husbands and feeling insecure and complaining about the food and so on. The authorities had to lay on something that could help these mothers abandoned out in the countryside. They weren't very good at being in the countryside. In fact they were pretty hopeless! But the local authorities had no choice; here was a trainload coming from the East End and they were just arriving with gas masks on strings round their necks and labels saying who they were. Some of the very young evacuated children had chewed their labels. I was in a kind of social work service, providing service for the children, and was asked to take responsibility for a group of evacuated children whom they considered 'unbilletable'. They had rather wild behaviour and were put in this large single dormitory and looked after by the ladies of the WVS. They were the 'good ladies of the manor' and they all wore uniforms of green overalls and cocked hats! They kept shouting out orders like, 'Come along now!' and 'Yes! Yes! Just here!'. I was fascinated by these 'come along' voices and wondered about what it felt like to be the children, isolated, lost and rushed. I found myself on both sides of the cultural and social fence. I had the accent and could talk like these posh ladies; I knew 'my way around' perfectly well. That was a help because it eased the tension and I was able to help the children without seeming to be a threat. Instead of there being one large dormitory, I divided the children up into small groups with an individual staff member in charge of each one. The children calmed down in weeks. I realise now that this experience gave me the idea of the Key Person approach.

Anita: So what happened after the war? I know that you said you worked in Italy and that is where you first tried out the idea of the Treasure Basket with babies.

Elinor: Yes! In 1946 I went to live with my husband, Guido, and son, Marco, who was then only a baby, in Trieste. When I first arrived I wondered how I was going to make a life there and how I would fit in. It was still under British occupation, so I was on both sides as it were. But I found Trieste to be a sophisticated town, not at all parochial; it was an international place with Catholics, Jews and Middle Eastern people.

I managed to get a job working in a state institution for illegitimate and abandoned children. Can you imagine it? I was working in an institution where 'Institute for Illegitimate Children' was written over the door. Luckily it wasn't run by the Church, otherwise I would not have been let in. Instead, there was a medical director in charge. He was an intelligent paediatrician, who had grown up in Vienna and had known Freud. His wife was a local magistrate, who had also been to the LSE. They were an open-minded couple and so there were a lot of possibilities for me. As I was willing to turn up punctually, bring play material, do the things I said I would, they took me on. It served me very well as I was able to take my son, Marco, with me.

It was there that I saw for the first time what Bowlby was describing in terms of mental and emotional deprivation. These babies in their cots were 'closed off' and when I offered them an object they reached, then drew their hands back. They just couldn't cope and I could see their level of fear and anxiety about touching, till eventually they managed to pick up an object with enormous caution. From a moment of negligence it became a moment of exchange. I then began to look around the environment for objects which could be held, sucked, banged to make a noise or moved by rolling. Those objects were my first collection so I did the Treasure Basket in a context. I've actually taken film of all that too.

The matron of the institution got the idea and so having play material as part of the routine of the day became the obvious thing to do. The staff began to have relationships with those babies too. We were able to reduce the crying, anxiety and all those negative things.

I then met Elda Scarzella, who began the idea of the Villagio della Madre e del Fanciullo. She had a new building in Milan and set up a coherent provision for mothers and their illegitimate babies. Under state provision mothers weren't allowed to keep their children, but the purpose of this new provision was to keep the mothers and babies together to foster their relationships. There were thousands of illegitimate children at that time. Through this work I was able to introduce play for hundreds of babies who, previously, had been cared for with no activity. I introduced the Treasure Basket because children in this category needed play more than anyone. I then began teaching and training in other institutions and my interest in group care has simply carried on to this day.

What Elinor failed to elaborate upon, in her usual modest way, was the fact that through her work she pioneered the transformation of childcare in Italy. Indeed, she continued to provide training in Italy and then in Spain until she was aged 90.

However, in 1955, Elinor returned to England, following the death of her husband, in order that her son, Marco, should receive an English secondary education. She was employed as an educational social worker for the London County Council until she decided to work as an educational consultant in several London boroughs. I met Elinor in 1981 at one of her training courses, when I was working as a play and language specialist in the local authority day nurseries for Hammersmith and Fulham. She became my mentor, friend and colleague from then until her death.

# CHAPTER 2

# How babies and children learn

What I propose to do in this chapter is to examine five aspects of learning. This will offer a basis from which to understand the value of the Treasure Basket for babies and Heuristic Play materials for toddlers. At the end of the chapter I will set out the EYFS principles, which are grouped into four distinct but complementary themes and you will see how they link with your own understanding of how children learn.

Heuristic Play is a descriptive term for the play of very young children, when they handle, explore and experiment with objects. Before children use and understand language, they are making sense of the world through their senses. First, they want to find out about the characteristics of the objects they are given by *mouthing* them (5–10 months). Then, they want to find out what they can do with the objects, by filling, emptying, piling, etc. (10–20 months). When children begin to understand and use language, they want to use their *imaginations* to find a functional use for the objects, such as when boxes become boats (20 months onwards).

Heuristic Play is creative and exploratory. What young children need is a range of natural and household materials from our real world, which offer breadth of experience and open-ended possibilities. However, it is not enough simply to offer children stimulating play materials. There must also be an understanding about how children learn, what stimulates that learning and what blocks it. For no learning is done in isolation; it is always in the context of a relationship.

## Five aspects of learning

1.  Involves having secure and loving relationships.
2.  Involves the balance between anxiety and curiosity to promote confident and responsible action.

3. Is about playing, taking risks and putting in effort.
4. Is about making mistakes.
5. Needs an appropriately stimulating environment.

## The importance of secure and loving relationships

Positive early relationships are considered so important to a child's learning, that they underpin the whole of the EYFS Framework (DfES 2007a) and Practice Guidance (DfES 2007b).

The 'Key Person approach' is being adopted in nurseries across the country to promote secure relationships for very young children, who are cared for in a group day care provision.

Peter Elfer *et al.* (2003: 18) describe the approach in this way:

> The Key Person approach is a way of working in nurseries in which the whole focus and organisation is aimed at enabling and supporting close attachments between individual children and individual nursery staff. The Key Person approach is an involvement, an individual and reciprocal commitment between a member of staff and a family. It is an approach that has clear benefits for all involved.

### Attachment theory and brain development

Bowlby's revelations, in the 1950s, about the importance of early secure relationships in the development of positive self-esteem, confidence and social responsibility led the development of his ideas into what became known as Attachment Theory. These ideas have been studied extensively, in particular by Winnicott (1964) and Ainsworth *et al.* (1978). With the advent of advanced brain-scanning techniques, there is renewed interest today in the connections between early positive relationships, brain development and learning.

### Love

Love and attentiveness from the first caregivers underpin a baby's desire and ability to learn. From a baby's point of view, if someone loves you and sees you as lovely, you feel lovely. If the closest adults are responsive, gentle and loving, then a baby's natural capacity to hope and love will grow. He will trust that the world will give him what he needs, which is vital for the development of self-esteem and personal worth.

Without love, the baby becomes anxious and does not reach out. If the baby does not reach out, he does not touch the world and remains locked in his 'own world', unable to develop into a competent and well-adjusted social person. For an extreme example of this, we only have to remind ourselves of the haunting images of Romanian orphans discovered in 1990, sitting or lying immobile in orphanage cots with completely blank expressions. Those children were neither able to play with objects nor were they able to make satisfactory relationships. Recent brain-scanning techniques reveal that these children's brains never developed the vital neuronal connections for making social relationships. They have social and learning difficulties to this very day.

Sue Gerhardt (2004: 38) cites the work of Chugani *et al.* (2001), stating:

> Work done with Romanian orphans has shown that those who were cut off from close bonds with an adult by being left in their cots all day, unable to make relationships, had a virtual black hole where their orbitofrontal cortex should be.

## Encouragement versus pressure

In almost all literature which describes children's play and learning there is reference to the need for children to be given encouragement. The *Collins English Dictionary* defines the word 'encourage' as follows:

- to give (someone) the confidence to do something;
- to stimulate someone by approval or help.

The word also suggests giving someone else the 'courage' to do something, but how we do that is worth reflecting on in the context of early play development. When babies and children feel safe and secure, they need no active encouragement as such. It is their natural instinct to play and socialise. Babies and young children get their encouragement from feeling safe and secure in their relationships, so it is important to build those first. It also means letting the child know that you are there for them, love and care about them and, very importantly, will not rush them. Encouragement also comes from trust. Children have a sixth sense about this and if you genuinely trust that they will be able to do something, then they magically often are!

Encouragement can feel like pressure when there is a deadline involved, like being rushed to complete some play activity before lunchtime or to say goodbye to a parent. Similarly, it is easy to inadvertently put children under pressure when they have to fit in with our 'planned activities' or when we 'take over' a child's interest. Recently, I visited a nursery and observed a small boy playing around with some wooden bricks. He was lining them up and then tried to build a tower. However, he was placing larger bricks on top of smaller ones and the tower kept falling down. One of the practitioners decided to 'help' by showing the boy how to put the larger bricks at the base. However, this little boy had not asked for the help. From this point on he 'went along' with the adult by watching what she was doing, but soon lost interest and moved away to another type of play material. The pleasure had clearly gone and the creative impulse had changed into feelings of 'ought' and 'should', which the little boy soon escaped from by moving away.

It is therefore important to be attentive and sensitive to the babies and children whenever you feel the urge to actively encourage, and then decide whether or not you would be intrusive or interfering. In essence, young children need no encouragement in their play.

## The balance between anxiety and curiosity

Curiosity is the driving force that underpins all learning. The ancient philosophy of Taoism is all about understanding life through an acceptance of (and insights about) its opposites. For example, we can never understand daylight, without having experienced darkness. We can never know and appreciate what real joy is unless we have experienced suffering. We can never really gain a sense of achievement until we know what it feels like to fail.

With that line of thinking, the 'other face' of curiosity is the experience of anxiety. Anxiety provides us with natural caution, which is a safety net, when we take on something new. As curiosity propels us outward, so anxiety holds us back. While the two are held in balance, it allows us to be both sensible and bold. New learning experiences then become infused with energy and excitement.

## Case study: Karen and the computer

Karen, a nursery manager in her early forties, described how she was initially very anxious about learning how to use a computer but, as she needed the skills for her job, she decided to go on a course. First of all she felt worried about who else would be attending and whether they might be more skilful than she was. Then she was anxious about what the tutor would be like. Would he or she explain things clearly enough or go through the stages slowly enough? Would she learn fast enough to impress her teenage son at home? Karen's anxiety was all in her imagination. It wasn't real; it was about *what might be.* However, her curiosity held equal sway in her imagination, because she wanted to see if she could succeed in the task of creating a Christmas card and already had an idea of *what it might look like.*

As it turned out, she discovered that learning how to use a computer was much easier than she had expected. Not only did she quickly become brave enough to experiment, but she also found that she learned the basic skills with relative ease. Her emotions shifted from nervous anticipation, lack of confidence, inadequacy and fear to those of excitement, feeling proud, happiness and a rush of energy. For, although new learning is tiring and can bring with it a sense of relief, it also gives energy and delight.

When asked which was the most significant feature that facilitated her learning, she said without hesitation, 'It was the tutor. He was so friendly and reassuring and patient and he always told me I was doing well, even when I got stuck. I didn't feel hurried and he let me make my own mistakes. I felt I could trust him.'

### When anxiety 'freezes' activity

It is very important to be sensitive towards the many babies and young children whose anxiety levels override their curiosity. Some of these children have such high levels of anxiety that they express it by becoming 'frozen' and immobile. They may hang on tightly to a trusted adult, sometimes crying in distress.

If a child has become 'paralysed' with anxiety and associated distress, he will not be able to play and be active. This means he will be unable to learn. If this anxiety becomes prolonged, then memories will be stored in the amygdala (the part of the brain that controls emotional response) that will trigger the 'flight' or 'freeze' response whenever faced with those kinds of situations again.

All children will be anxious when they first leave the family home to be looked after by someone else, whether by a childminder, an unfamiliar relative or in a nursery setting of some kind. It is important for the caregiver to build up trust in the relationship, by being patient and comforting. The child needs to be allowed time for observation before participation. Sensitive encouragement can then be offered when you are confident that the child has begun to relax.

We live in such a frantic and fast-moving world that it is often difficult to slow down to a child's emotional pace. However, we need to recognise, acknowledge and respond to the child's levels of anxiety and curiosity, so he can develop the capacity for self-regulation.

## When curiosity can lead to danger

If the anxiety/curiosity balance is tipped the other way, then you will see children who seem to have no fear of anything at all. These are the children whose outgoing personalities and curiosity can lead them into all sorts of unexpected danger. Their conviction that adults will step in and protect them means that they are not properly developing their regulatory levels of caution. While it is a delight to observe the confidence, humour and enthusiasm of these young children, the efforts of the adults need to focus on providing clear boundaries and sensitive guidance.

## When anxiety looks like curiosity

There are also other children who appear to have no regard for their own safety and may even be aggressive towards toys or other children. They may present as having little anxiety in the way they explore their environment without seeking reassurance from the adults. However, these children do not have the anxiety/curiosity balance in a healthy state of equilibrium at all. These children are presenting with the 'anxious/avoidant' type of insecure attachment relationship described by Mary Ainsworth *et al.* (1978). In fact, if you closely observe children of this type, you will find that their behaviour does not actually demonstrate curiosity about their environment; rather, they are seeking to avoid social contact with others to alleviate their anxiety. Such children will need a lot of very sensitive handling to help them develop the trust to make the secure relationships they need to release the impulse to become genuinely curious about their surroundings.

For a good balance between anxiety and curiosity, the baby or young child needs to:

- have a secure and loving relationship with both parent and caregiver;
- experience sympathetic understanding;
- receive patient and non–intrusive support;
- receive gentle handling – allowing close proximity to the adult (sitting on her lap) and remaining still and undisturbed;
- be shown the play experiences on offer, but without feeling pressurised to participate;
- be allowed to 'take the lead' about whether to simply observe, get closer or actually touch something;
- be told in a reassuring way what is happening and what is going to happen;
- feel confident that his expressed delight (when he has taken part in some activity) can be shared;
- experience the benefits of supportive, positive and open communication between the parent and the caregiver.

## Play, risks and effort

### Play

The most fundamental aspect of childhood is play. 'Play' is one of those generic terms, which is used by everyone to describe what children do. In many cultures there is no term for 'play' as such, but the Western world has become so curious about, and bound up with, children and their development, that play has become a whole new focus of interest in its own right. There has been an enormous amount of study and research into children's play over the past two to three decades.

There are also different views and attitudes about children's play and their activities. Many people use the term 'play' in a derogatory way. 'Oh! He is only playing', or 'Will you stop playing and come and do something more useful?' Others view children's play as intrusive, out of control and in some way unnecessary. There are those who hold a rather sentimental view of play and see the activities of children merely as sweet, funny and cute.

However, playing is the most vital activity in life. For it is through playing that we learn everything that is truly useful in our lives. We learn about giving and taking, we learn about the complex nature of our environment, we learn how to solve problems, we learn how to relate to others in a mutually satisfying way and we are always able to be creative. In short, play not only teaches us how to learn, it is the magic at the heart of childhood and the secret of a satisfying life.

## What is play?

So what is play? Play is spontaneous self-chosen activity, which is at times riotously carefree and, at others, earnestly careful. Play is also about sustained thinking, being creative and imaginative and engaging in vibrant energy. It is unpredictable, 'on the edge', out of the 'comfort zone' and can sometimes be downright 'dodgy'. If children are asked to do something and they act out of obedience (even if it is *called* play) then they are not really playing. They are participating in a directed activity. However, this can turn into play the moment a child starts to do what he wants.

In a day care or nursery context, adults regularly encourage children to play in certain ways. A child may be encouraged to paint or to play with sand. This is fine, so long as the adult allows the child to get absorbed independently or choose to move away. Children and adults can enter into play together, when the activity is genuinely spontaneous and equal between the two parties and not simply with the adult taking the lead. This can often be seen in situations like playing with dough, sandcastle building, play wrestling, painting or when playing games with rules such as ball games, card games and board games.

## Risks

Play can also be described as 'precarious' because children take themselves to the 'edge' creatively, physically, emotionally and mentally. Children seek to take risks because, through their play, they are constantly trying out new experiences, while at the same time, overlaying them with what is familiar. We can see this behaviour physically when a child climbs higher up a tree than he has ever done before or when a toddler builds his tallest tower of bricks. We see it when the 'den' becomes more and more elaborate as new ideas are expressed and tried out. We see it when our children set ever-more complex rules for their games of conquest.

When children are fully absorbed in their play, they will, quite naturally, move from repeating something familiar to entering the 'unknown'. For older children (from about five years and upwards) it is the planning, the setting up and the organisation of rules, which creates far greater pleasure and generates much more energy than the product or the organised game at the end. Many a time I have seen tremendous creative energy being put into setting up something like a ship, a house, a farmyard or a space station and then, when the creation is complete, the 'game' somehow dies and some new idea develops, leaving the construction abandoned.

Although it is quite natural for children to take risks in their play, there can be exceptions for children who have learning or emotional difficulties or for those coming into a new situation. A feature of these children is that they choose to stay with what is familiar and can often become resistant to new learning. They do not want to venture out of the 'comfort zone' and leave behind what is familiar. When children are afraid of risk-taking they need to be helped to feel safe through adult reassurance, patience and guidance to ease them into the 'unknown'.

## Effort

Children intuitively know that learning is about effort and doing for its own sake. They demonstrate it to us by their determination to master simple tasks, which, for them, are new and tantalising. They are constantly setting themselves challenges. On the one hand, they move heavy objects about, like furniture or heavy bags and boxes, and yet, on the other hand, carefully sort out fine objects like beads or tiny pebbles at the seashore. They demonstrate powers of concentration and a level of perseverance that many of us lose before we reach the age of ten. Adults unwittingly kill off the natural learning instincts in young children by interference, too much assistance, constant criticism or simple lack of patience.

## Creative tension

There is also an interesting misconception that play is all to do with pleasure. It goes without saying that play does give enormous pleasure and children choose to repeat experiences because they are stimulating, make them happy or are exciting.

However, when children become really absorbed, there is often tension. This can be very uncomfortable for the adults, but it is in fact part of the creative and learning process. If a child is experimenting with a new idea or form, he will be edgy, excitable and tense. There may be chaos all around, in the physical objects or in his mind. But this is an essential part of the creative process, from which comes the exhilarating energy release. Parents and caregivers need to be sensitive and attentive to children's emotional states to be able to tell when the heightened expressed emotions are actually part of the creative process or when the play has got out of hand and a child is crying out for help.

## The paradox of failure

Experiencing failure is one of the most significant barriers to learning.

You can only effectively learn when you experience failure.

Both these statements are accurate and correct. Both these statements are 'right'. But how can they be? Surely only one is right because they are stating such opposites? One must be 'wrong'. However, it is the concepts of 'wrongness' and 'rightness' and how we experience and deal with them, which is at the base of this confusion and paradox.

Failure is about not managing to do what you intended to do. The experience is usually disappointing and frustrating, but it can also be viewed as interesting. You can look at it as useful feedback or information, or you can view yourself as a failure and in some way feel inferior or not good enough.

We need to remember and remind ourselves that many of the most important scientific discoveries have been made 'by chance', when the scientist has 'failed' to do what he intended to do and discovered something else instead, such as the discovery of penicillin.

### Competence in the face of failure

Babies and very young children feel perfectly competent in the face of what we might see as 'failure'. They need to because, otherwise, they would not have the motivation to try over and over again to crawl, walk, put on a pair of socks, use a spoon or hold a pencil to make a mark with it.

Failure to achieve what you originally intend gives you the opportunity to modify how you do something in order to achieve your intention, so you can feel even more competent and in control. It can also give you the opportunity for an entirely new idea or new way of doing something. A fluke immediate success may give a momentary good feeling, but it does not engender real confidence or competence because you do not know how to repeat such success. Through failing to do as you intend, you can discover that there may be other possibilities and avenues to achieve the end result you seek, and this will give an even greater sense of competence.

For example, in primary schools, the teaching of early numeracy skills at Key Stage 1 and 2 (5–11 years) is now all about 'playing around with numbers', seeing how many different ways you can manipulate numbers to get the same result. Through this approach to learning, the children get an overall 'feel' for numbers. They are not relying on their memories for learning one particular method or process.

### When fear of failure creates a barrier to learning

A competent learner is someone who allows himself to be totally immersed in the activity, process or experience for its own sake. A competent learner feels secure in his relationships with others.

However, it is the fear of failure, which becomes the barrier to learning when a child (or, indeed, an adult) focuses their emotional and mental energy on worrying about what someone else might think of him if he did fail. The child is not able to fully engage his energy in the activity for its own sake (whatever the outcome) because he is more focused on the response of someone else than on the enjoyment of the activity. Failure becomes associated with fear.

There is the fear that someone else might be disappointed with you, mock or humiliate you. There is the fear that someone may tell you off or disapprove of you. Even worse, there is the fear that you might be ignored altogether. So, instead of enjoying the learning experience for its own sake or for the possibilities it might offer, the child becomes distracted through the fear of failing to satisfy someone else.

In my 28 years of being an educational psychologist and working with children with special needs, I have found that, whenever there has been a concern about a child's learning, that child has shown strong feelings of fear of failure. This can come across in various ways, such as stubbornness or cheating, refusal to try new things, repeated requests for reassurance from trusted adults, tearfulness, destruction of whatever has been created and so on. Sadly, the primary difficulty, which may be a sensory impairment, dyslexia or a syndrome (such as Down's or Asperger's), becomes secondary as the *new* primary learning difficulty becomes the fear of failure.

### When the caregiver's 'fear of failure' influences a child's learning

Although very young children are naturally comfortable with failure as part of their daily learning experience, there are increasing numbers presenting with anxiety and stress, which is inhibiting the natural flow of their activity.

So obsessed have we become by setting goals, measuring and monitoring progress and looking for desired outcomes that we, the caregivers, have become frightened that if a child is not 'making the grade', then in some sense *we* are the failures. Our anxiety then rubs off on the children and a vicious cycle is set in motion where child and parent or caregiver are playing desperate games of pleasing one another and so lose sight of the natural impulses to try things out, whatever the mistakes on the way. For learning is about persevering in the face of things not working out as you want them to and experiencing reassurance from a beloved adult, so frustration and disappointment can be contained and managed.

It is important to be clear about our views on failure, success and progress so that our attitudes towards children's learning can be put in perspective.

## An appropriately stimulating environment

All babies and children need a stimulating environment in order to feed their natural curiosity and desire to learn. The natural environment, with its abundance of trees, fruits and flowers, grass, stones and shells, insects, birds and animals, puddles and streams, provides endless fascination for the young child. The domestic environment of cooking utensils, ornaments, furnishings, clothes, books, magazines, CDs and DVDs is another world of infant interest.

The challenge for us, as caregivers, is to find ways to offer these environments in safe and manageable 'chunks'. Later in this book, the Treasure Basket and Heuristic Play will be described and explained as two powerful and stimulating approaches that embrace our natural and domestic world, while remaining manageable and safe.

## The Early Years Foundation Stage: a principled approach

### A unique child

Every child is a competent learner from birth who can be resilient, capable, confident and self-assured.

(DfES 2007b: 5)

### Positive relationships

Children learn to be strong and independent from a base of loving and secure relationships with parents and/or a Key Person.

(DfES 2007b: 5)

### Enabling environments

The environment plays a key role in supporting and extending children's development and learning.

(DfES 2007b: 5)

### Learning and development

Children develop and learn in different ways and at different rates and all areas of learning and development are equally important and interconnected.

(DfES 2007b: 5)

# CHAPTER 3

# The beginning of sensory and physical development

## The brain is a neural wonder

Although parents and developmental specialists have guessed it, the neuro-scientists are now proving it. Our brains are not fixed; they are malleable and full of potential. Indeed, babies create their own brain function by using their senses, moving about, responding to affection and communicating.

When a baby is born, his brain has approximately 100 billion neurons (electrical nerve cells), which is about the same number as the stars that make up the Milky Way. However, it is the sensory, emotional and physical activities, which 'switch on' the electrical activity, creating neural connections in the brain that make thinking and learning happen. The more we use the brain, the more it grows and is of use to us.

### Making sense of the world

During the first few weeks of life, a baby is making sense of the world through his senses, allowing discrimination between what is familiar and what is new. For example, a baby will show recognition by smiling at a familiar face and will feed comfortably with a familiar nursing caregiver. Sue Gerhardt (2004: 44) succinctly explains this discrimination as the 'shaping' of a baby's brain when she says:

> Out of the chaotic overproduction of connections within the brain, pat-terns start to emerge. The most frequent and repetitive experiences start to form well-trodden pathways, whilst those connections that lie unused begin to be pruned away. The brain takes shape.

Life for the growing baby is a sensory journey of discovery, as every day he learns to apply the powers of discrimination by using his senses. If a baby feels safe and loved he will take delight in recognising more and more of his daily experiences.

---

**Case study: James and the TV 'soap', *Coronation Street***

Helen continued her life in a fairly ordinary manner throughout her first pregnancy with James. This included going to work during the day and relaxing in front of the television in the evenings.

Helen's favourite programme was *Coronation Street* and she made sure that she never missed an episode of this popular 'soap opera', which is broadcast most days of the week.

When her son, James, was born, she brought him home from hospital and made sure he was comfortable and settled before she sat down to watch *Coronation Street*. On came the familiar music of the theme tune and, much to her surprise, James suddenly became alert and responsive. Although James was only a few days old, he had nevertheless 'heard' and 'recognised' the music. This was because, as a foetus, he had been 'hearing' the theme music regularly for the previous four months or so, when his mother was quiet and relaxed. Now, Helen was witnessing James's desire to make sense of the world of sound, by his active 'noticing' of what he was recognising from the chaos of all the noises flooding his newborn ears.

**The mouthing stage**

As a baby begins to reach out to grasp and hold objects for himself, he is taking the first step towards physical control of his surroundings. When the baby seeks to pick up objects and explore them, the first thing he usually does is put the object straight in his mouth. This is described as the 'mouthing stage'. It is the first stage when adults naturally want to give babies things to 'play with' and usually begins at around the age of four to five months old.

Some caregivers are uncomfortable about babies putting objects in their mouths, because they interpret this as being dirty or unsafe. However, from the baby's point of view, until he begins to grab things, the physical world has only been experienced as a 'virtual reality', except for the experience of feeding. It makes sense then, that when a baby picks up something unfamiliar, he will want to 'test it out' in his mouth, which is the only part of his body where he has had direct contact with an object (nipple or teat).

The senses of smell and taste, as well as the experience of having something in the mouth, provide very powerful and primitive stimuli that last throughout our lives. We only have to think of the pleasure of eating chocolate, the smell of perfume, the feel of a soft towel against the cheek or the habits of smoking cigarettes and chewing gum to remind us of the potency of these senses.

### Grasping happens before picking up

At first, a baby does not have the ability to pick up and put down things at will. He might see something that he wants to touch, but is unable to direct his hand accurately. The baby's arm will move about in a waving motion and, if his fingers so much as brush against something, they will automatically 'grasp' at that thing.

This also means that a baby might inadvertently grasp an object of which he may be totally unaware. He also is unable to release his grasp on an object or drop it at will until he is about six months old.

> ## Case study: John is introduced to a selection of objects for the first time
>
> John is not yet sitting up independently, but he is being supported by his key caregiver on a soft carpeted floor. In front of him is a small basket of objects, which include two bangles, a pine cone, a length of linked key rings, a piece of fabric and a small leather purse. Both arms wave about in excited fashion and suddenly both of John's hands land on the edge of the basket and grip tightly. With a sudden jerk, one of John's hands becomes disengaged from the basket edge and touches two bangles, which are instantly grasped. John looks intently at the objects and his whole body seems to stiffen in excitement. John's caregiver adjusts her position, to ensure that John is comfortable, but remains quiet and patient.
>
> One of the bangles falls from John's fingers as he loosens his grip on the basket with his other hand and both arms begin to wave about again. John's gaze does not lose its intensity. The hand with the single bangle brushes against a piece of cloth and his two smallest fingers catch a corner of it. For a few moments, John is holding the bangle and piece of cloth in one hand, before it is suddenly released from his grasp. John is not able to pick up and release objects at will yet, but he is clearly very interested in the objects and is intentionally reaching out for them, even though his movements are clumsy.
>
> This play continues for a further ten minutes and John's caregiver shows quiet and attentive interest throughout that period. She allows John's intent interest to be maintained without intrusion or direction.
>
> (From the film *I Don't Need Toys* (Anita M. Hughes 1991))

## The importance of using hands

If a child has not been given the opportunity to use his hands, he will become lazy and sad. Exploration and learning must initially come through the hands. It is a first point of contact with the outside world and is the only natural way forward. If a child cannot do what he is compelled to do from within, he will become sad and lifeless and, with that, lazy. Children who have used their hands develop their intellectual skills and their strength of character as they make their mark on the world.

The seated baby is only interested in the physical characteristics of the objects he encounters. As a toddler, when he is familiar with what things are like, he will be ready to understand and learn about how he can manipulate the objects, in preparation for learning what things are called, what their functions are and how they can be skillfully used (from 20 months).

## Toys normally on offer to the baby at the mouthing stage

When babies reach the mouthing stage, the kind of playthings commonly offered to stimulate interest, are manufactured plastic rattles and soft toys. Rattles are usually brightly coloured and made to resemble currently popular cartoon characters, like Winnie the Pooh or common objects like a train. However, rattles are often too large for a young baby to hold and the images or shapes portrayed are totally meaningless to him.

Soft toys may initially be sucked and then become a source of comfort, but their 'play value' does not really become apparent until children are beginning to use language and gain a sense of themselves as separate from others and the soft toys become 'inanimate others'.

### Selling for visual impact

The manufacturers and distributors of plastic rattles and toys are marketing and selling their products to appeal initially to the adults. As adults, we are tempted to buy things because of the way they look and this goes for babies' toys as well. Although we do use all our senses, we live in a largely visual world.

To illustrate the current interest in visual stimulation, we have only to think of the various kinds of television programmes that are regularly viewed by millions of people. There are programmes about buying, rebuilding or decorating houses, which place the emphasis on colour schemes, light and style. The gardening programmes have expanded from simply how to grow plants to selecting the style of decking, the colour of paint for the fence or the shape of terracotta pots. Food programmes similarly emphasise the importance of the appearance of the food on the plate as well as its flavour.

### Plastic is dull and disappointing

When a baby's hands are large enough to hold the rattle and put it in his mouth, he discovers that, although the rattles may *look* different, one plastic rattle tastes, smells and feels very much like another.

To our adult eyes, the rattles are bright and fun, because we are choosing them for their appearance. However, the baby is primarily using the senses of touch, smell and taste to explore and find out about the characteristics of the rattles. For him, the rattles soon become limiting, dull and disappointing. It is rather like being offered baked beans on toast for breakfast, lunch and supper every day of the week.

We often forget that, until a baby can move about independently, he is marooned in one place and is very much at the mercy of the people around him in terms of what he will be given to play with and explore.

# CHAPTER 4

# The Treasure Basket

## 'What is the object like?'

## What is the object like?

The only way to get some sense of the deep satisfaction that babies experience when they are handling objects is to 'get in touch' with the feel, essence and energy of a range of objects for yourself.

A very useful way to do this is to try out the following exercise. After collecting eight objects and an open dish or small basket, set aside ten minutes of uninterrupted time to carry it out.

### Exercise to try

1.  Select a number of objects with very different physical characteristics. Here are some suggestions:

    - a large pebble
    - a leather purse
    - a chain and plug
    - a pine cone
    - a new (unused) shaving brush
    - a small glass vanilla essence bottle
    - a fresh lemon
    - a toothbrush.

2.  Place all the objects in an open dish or small basket. Select the objects one at a time, feeling them individually in your hands, with your eyes shut. In this way the dominant visual sense, which is usually key in forming our judgements, is taken away. For example, supposing you picked out the toothbrush and first of all 'looked' at it. Maybe the

thought, 'What an odd/inappropriate object to give a baby' might cross your mind or 'Oh my goodness! Did I clean my teeth this morning?'. Or, 'That reminds me, I must buy some toothpaste later today!' could intrude and distract you.

These thoughts are simply judgements and questions, reflecting into the past and projecting into the future. There is nothing wrong with them, but they get in the way of experiencing the essence of 'toothbrushness'.

3.  Instead, take the toothbrush and close your eyes. Allow your fingers to explore the strange, uneven shape of the long handle, some of it smooth and slightly warm in the hand. Notice the strange rubbery ridges at the bottom of the handle end and enjoy the 'ticklish' sensation of the bristles. Are the bristles stiff? Do they spring back in your fingers as you flick them? Notice the rigidity of the handle and compare it with the flexibility of the bristles. Is the toothbrush heavy or lightweight? Just notice how it feels in your hand. Does the toothbrush smell of anything? Maybe, if it is a clean, but used, brush, it has the traces of a minty smell? Notice how you are feeling about this object. Does it trigger any emotional response? Maybe it is comforting, maybe it produces a sense of agitation or urgency, or it may even feel repulsive to you.

4.  Continue this exercise with the rest of the objects. When you have finished, you will probably have gained some sense of the 'ness' of the objects, whether it is 'stoneness', 'shellness', 'woodness' or 'glassness'. This is precisely the experience the baby has when exploring objects with his hands and mouth.

## Case study: reactions of a group of nursery workers who did this exercise at a training workshop

(For this exercise, the people did not know in advance what the objects would be.)

*   'I felt nervous every time I touched a new object. Not knowing was scary and exciting.'

*   'I made a kind of relationship with the first object (which was a metal compact case) and enjoyed its cool smoothness. It was a pleasant relief when the case had done the full circle and came back to me. However, I also experienced a strange sense of disappointment even intrusion,

because it was no longer cold. It felt warm in my hands from the other people having handled it.'

- 'At first I wondered what it was, but when I brought it up to my cheek, I could suddenly see my grandfather clearly in my mind, in the bathroom shaving. I loved my grandfather so much and I used to secretly watch him going through his shaving ritual. Handling and smelling that shaving brush today brought it all back to me. It made me feel sad because I am no longer a little girl and he is no longer alive. But I also got a really strong sense of connection and a warm feeling of love.'

- 'I shall never forget the sensual pleasure I experienced when I handled the leather wallet. The smell was fabulous and as my fingers explored the hidden compartments, I was transported into a different world. I somehow wasn't here at all. I could never have believed that something so commonplace and familiar could have such a profound effect on me.'

## Are the objects safe?

Although the rational mind can quickly grasp how a variety of objects can offer huge satisfaction and learning possibilities for the sitting baby, the emotional mind will put up obstacles. One of the most important duties of a caregiver is to ensure the safety of a baby and so one wants to make sure that the objects on offer are safe.

However, there are *no clear criteria* about what constitutes *safe*. Everyone has their own *opinions* based on their own *experiences*. There is a physiological explanation for this, which comes from the part of the brain called the amygdala. Daniel Goleman (1996) called the amygdala the 'emotional sentinel' of the brain. This is because any experiences we have had that suggest danger or threat are remembered in this part of the brain. When faced once again with a similar situation again, the amygdala springs to life causing us to *react* before we have had a chance to *think*.

To give a typical example of the amygdala at work, a person will rush to save a complete stranger from an accident (like drowning, being burned or crushed), risking their own life in the process. When asked how they could have been so brave, such a person usually says they never even thought about it at the time.

When I meet someone, who has an instant reaction of anxiety relating to a Treasure Basket object, it is usually based on some past experience that, either directly or indirectly, involved being hurt.

### Common fears

#### Objects that might break (like glass)

An obvious candidate to elicit a negative reaction is a small glass bottle. We all know that glass can break, and that if you cut yourself on broken glass it could be lethal. However, if you feel comfortable giving a baby a small, thick glass bottle it is probably because you have been able to 'reason' that it would be almost impossible for a young baby to smash a small, tough bottle. At least, this would be so when the baby is sitting on a soft surface at ground level, does not yet have the strength or coordination to throw and is being constantly supervised by an attentive adult.

When I ask those, who 'could not possibly give a baby a small glass bottle' about past experiences they *all* give the same replies. They have either been directly injured by broken glass or have been frightened early in life by an important caregiver communicating their fears. These experiences have been remembered in the amygdala and 'fear response' has been instantly evoked.

#### Objects that might be sharp

As with the fears associated with glass, there are many materials which could potentially be sharp and could therefore possibly cut or scratch a baby, such as a pine cone, the rim of a metal bell or a shell. Many people reject the idea of an object before putting it to the test in a safe environment. Babies are extraordinarily careful, when exploring and mouthing objects, especially if the object is unfamiliar. However, care needs to be taken to keep the materials well-maintained and replace them when necessary. Shells, for example, can become brittle and snap and then be dangerously sharp. However, it is denying a baby a sensory experience to withhold an object in case it becomes sharp. It is better to be vigilant and act responsibly if a baby is getting into difficulty.

#### Objects with handles (spoons, brushes, whisks, etc.)

Many people fear that a baby could push the handle too far down his throat, or might fall on the handle and choke.

A caregiver once gave a graphic description of the source of her fear:

> I know where my fear comes from, when I was a little girl, I was playing on the back of the sofa and fell. I had a pencil in my hand, which went in my ear and caused me a horrible injury. I can't even bear to think of my baby playing with anything with a handle.

Whatever one's emotional reactions or fears, all babies will soon be feeding themselves with a spoon, using a toothbrush or hairbrush and, indeed, handling all manner of tools and toys with handles. In fact, all the objects in the Treasure Basket are likely to be picked up and handled at some stage or another. So, it becomes very important to examine the source of any instant anxiety and see if thinking rationally about it helps to dissolve it.

### Objects that are small

Choking is a common fear that people have when they are considering their choices of objects for the Treasure Basket. However, there is a product on the market, called a 'choke tester'. I can recommend this product to those who would feel more comfortable 'knowing' for certain that the object could not go through this simple cylindrical device, and that it would therefore not fit down a baby's throat.

It is interesting to observe that many people compensate for this fear by putting objects into the Treasure Basket which are far too large. For example, I have seen loofahs of about 20 centimetres long, when a length of 4 centimetres is about right.

## The benefits of being able to manage one's fears responsibly

It is good if you are able to identify the source of your anxiety (about any objects) and to understand there is a physiological reason for your emotional reaction. It helps you to be able to consider your fears rationally. Then you can think about and talk through the possible benefits of offering such objects to a baby.

For example, glass is deliciously cold, when first handled. It is smooth to touch, with interesting bumps and ridges, like the screw top rim or the 'hallmark' base. You can see through it and its transparency catches the light and sparkles in the sunshine. Sometimes it even reflects the rainbow spectrum of colours. Even the cylindrical shape, with the narrow neck, offers wonderful satisfaction for handling. There is so much sensory richness to a simple little bottle, which can all too easily be perceived as a threat and rejected.

The greater the variety of objects on offer to a baby in a Treasure Basket, the richer and more stimulating it will be.

## Communicating our anxieties to babies

The strength of the relationship which caregivers share with babies is connected to love and 'emotional attunement'. This attunement is never one-way. As we pick up the emotions of the babies and adjust the way we respond to them, so they do with us.

If there is an object in the Treasure Basket that causes you anxiety, you will inadvertently communicate that anxiety to the baby. This may be expressed as an extra sense of vigilance or a sinking feeling that 'something' might happen. The focus is less on being in tune with the baby's delight, apprehension or satisfaction and more on managing your own emotions of distrust, anxiety and tension.

What then happens is that the baby *picks up* your anxiety (even though he does not understand it) and responds with an element of distraction. The play loses its spontaneity, its free-flowing, but concentrated attention and pleasurable satisfaction and becomes rather more awkward and unsatisfactory, because the baby is now tuning in to your feelings. He then may even begin to associate the negative feelings he has picked up from you with the objects in front of him. He begins to form the most primitive type of pre-verbal judgement.

Similarly, if you feel comfortable with, interested in and confident about the objects in the Treasure Basket, you are giving the baby 'permission' to feel the same. He will not consciously understand this, but he will be developing attitudes and a relationship towards his environment, namely, that it is fine to explore and to be curious.

It is therefore of paramount importance to examine your own level of trust and confidence, both in the relationship you have with the baby, and with the objects you offer as playthings. Learning is most potent when there is mutual satisfaction between caregiver and baby in the experiences that are shared.

## Case study: the story of the defensive mother, the determined baby and the nutcracker

Hannah was the teenage mother of eight-month-old Ryan, living in a hostel, but determined to give her son the 'best start' in life. Hannah was required to attend parenting workshops as part of the agreement in her accommodation.

On this particular occasion, she was introduced to the Treasure Basket. During the first part of the session, Ryan and three other babies were being supervised in another room to allow the mothers to participate without distraction. However, for Hannah, the idea of giving her baby something like a shell or a metal whisk was outrageous and she became very agitated and defensive. She saw the objects as disgusting, inferior and unsafe, in comparison to the expensive and glossy plastic toys she had seen in the shops. She told me that she wanted the best for her baby and had clearly equated price with value.

After some discussion, the babies were then brought into the group and sat down beside the basket. Ryan was a large baby for his age, with wide and sparkling eyes brimming with his mother's same determination and energy. It was as if he could not believe his luck when he saw the Treasure Basket! He had never seen anything like it before and immediately lent forward and picked up a heavy metal nutcracker. The weight of it took him by surprise and he somehow swung his arm in a way that meant the nutcracker hit him quite hard on the forehead.

In a flash, Hannah pulled an angry expression and said, 'See! These objects are dangerous and unsuitable. I told you I was right'.

In the very same moment, she lent forward and scooped her surprised baby in her arms, pulling the nutcracker out of his hands as she did so. Far from this action providing comfort, Ryan began to cry out loudly. Nothing would pacify him until he was returned to the Treasure Basket with the nutcracker. From that moment, Ryan spent a further 45 minutes totally engrossed in the objects, without any further incident.

Hannah could not believe her eyes. Usually Ryan demanded her attention and wanted stimulation the whole time. She had never seen him so occupied and calm at the same time. Now it was the mother, as well as the baby, who was captivated by the objects.

The initial 'hurt', while a shock at the time, was not serious. Ryan had never seen or touched anything quite like this before. It was shiny, cold, smooth, heavy and moved in his hands. It was new, exciting and different. Babies regularly express distress, not only through physical hurt, but also from confusion, fear of abandonment, tiredness, etc. In the safe presence of his mother and the calm atmosphere of the group, Ryan instantly wanted to explore more and to try out a whole range of objects he had never seen, let alone handled, before. As Hannah felt more comfortable and confident, so Ryan's concentration and interest grew.

By the end of the session, Hannah decided that she wanted to create her own Treasure Basket, which she later went on to do and became an enthusiastic advocate with her peer group.

## Playing with the Treasure Basket is a 'non-social' activity

Although an attentive adult is always present, when a baby is playing with objects in the Treasure Basket and the baby may copy or reach out to another baby nearby, the activity is fundamentally non-social. This is because the baby is gaining pleasure and satisfaction from exploring the objects for their own sake.

The pleasure is not dependent on another person in the form of an interaction, such as when playing a 'peek-a-boo' game, tickling or feeding. It is the objects themselves which provide the source of interest and not the way someone else uses the objects. Indeed, if an adult handles the objects with a baby, the play *changes* into a social form of play. While this is not 'wrong', it needs to be recognised that the play is different and the qualities described and the way the baby learns with the Treasure Basket will be less potent.

## There is social interaction at the Treasure Basket

While the baby's exploratory activity with objects is non-social, there will, nevertheless, be social interaction if two or three babies share the same basket. This is because human nature is basically sociable and we are all curious about what others do, have or how they respond, even at as young an age as six to nine months old.

Babies do not engage in social play at this early age, as they do not understand the idea of sharing and are unable to communicate their intentions except at a very primitive level. However, social interaction certainly takes place. It is common to see that if one baby shakes an object, then a second baby will copy this activity by shaking another object in his hand. Babies will also exchange glances and smiles with each other as well as seeking to touch each other. They also begin to acquire a sense of possession and there can be small 'tussles' as two babies compete with each other for the same object.

Similarly, there is often an exchange of glances and smiles between the caretaker and the baby, although this happens less than between the babies themselves. This is because the adult caretaker is not touching the objects and so there is no direct distraction or competition.

## The importance of choice

The most significant feature of our Western way of life is the fact we have so much choice. Everywhere we turn we are faced with choices. At one time, we could go to a teashop and buy a pot of tea. Now we are faced with a choice of fruit teas, herbal teas, spiced teas, Indian, Himalayan, Chinese, small cups, large cups or mugs.

Every aspect of our lives now involves making choices, from selecting who supplies the electricity to your home, which bag of frozen chips to buy, to whether there is a television programme you might wish to view. The most obvious area, which involves seemingly infinite choice, is what you might select on the Internet. Choices confront us every day of our lives.

Choice implies selection, variety and possibility. Variety implies characteristics and description. By being able to select, one is not only embracing variety, but there is also the choice to 'act', rather than simply 'react' to desires and impulses. The ability to select has become a fundamental requirement in this day and age and underpins all decision–making. Being able to make decisions in a world of choices is the gateway to being in control of one's life. When you feel in control of your life, you can create the world you want. If we look around and examine the people who are confident, happy and successful, they are those who are able to make and act upon their decisions.

## How the Treasure Basket promotes learning

### The Treasure Basket offers choice

The principle of the Treasure Basket is unique in that it is a way of consciously offering a baby the experience of making choices. Babies are naturally curious about the world and the more experiences they are

*Figure 4.1* Babies around a Treasure Basket are totally absorbed as they examine, handle, mouth and shake the different objects

offered, where they can choose, the more those experiences will feed their curiosity.

The question is often asked about whether it is too overwhelming for a baby to be given such a large choice of objects in a Treasure Basket (between 80 and 100). The answer is definitely no! Babies have absolutely no difficulty about being offered a large range of objects if they have:

- the choice of *which* ones to select for themselves;
- the choice of *whether* they pick the objects up or not;
- the choice about *when* to pick up any objects.

Objects from a Treasure Basket are only overwhelming if the adult takes charge and hands the baby objects, dangles them in front of his face, tickles him with objects and generally intrudes on the baby's 'space'.

It is the large variety of objects all in one place in a Treasure Basket that actually stimulates curiosity and interest. We often forget that, until a baby can move about independently, his choices are limited to what the people around him will give him to play with.

## The Treasure Basket promotes concentration skills

One of the most striking features of providing the seated baby with a rich variety of objects in a Treasure Basket is how it promotes the development of concentration. In society today, we are bombarded with such a range of distracting stimuli, that it is difficult to have the opportunity to maintain concentration at any one thing for long.

The distinguishing feature of children with good learning skills is their ability to concentrate and to stick at a task they have set themselves. A baby will concentrate and be absorbed in the objects from a Treasure Basket for up to an hour. Although a baby will be affected by fatigue, physical discomfort or hunger, once all those needs have been met, his powers of concentration as he sits by a Treasure Basket are truly remarkable.

In fact, I would go so far as to say that this intense concentration is the most striking feature of the baby's behaviour when playing with objects from a Treasure Basket. It is truly satisfying to baby and caregiver alike. The shared pleasure through glances, smiles and gestures between a baby and his caregiver prolongs the time he will be happily engaged with the objects and intensifies the levels of a baby's interest and concentration.

## The Treasure Basket facilitates conceptual learning

Through the repeated handling of a variety of objects, babies learn many abstract concepts, which are not apparent to most adults. Adults often simply see the objects as being put in the mouth, fiddled with, moved about, shaken, banged against other objects or dropped.

Babies learn a range of concepts to do with the physical qualities of objects, such as coldness, smoothness, heaviness and prickliness. They also begin to recognise that some objects are rigid and others move about between their fingers. They notice that some objects are hollow and others are solid. They experience the transparency of glass and the reflective nature of shiny metal. They experience the fact that some objects change temperature as you hold them and some do not. The temperature of glass and metal in one's hands changes very quickly, whereas wood, cork or fabric does not change very much. A baby discovers that some material has a strong scent, such as leather, rubber or a lemon, whereas the scents of wicker, bristle or stone are less potent.

Children who have had the experience of handling, mouthing and experimenting with objects understand these complex concepts long before they have the language to express them or the maturity to use and manipulate them. Indeed, language can best be learned through direct experience. The Treasure Basket gives a baby, at the sitting stage, the opportunity to handle and explore as many different objects as possible to enrich their experience, stimulate their curiosity and provide the foundations of language development.

Language development is a fundamental aspect of communication. Children's first words largely reflect their direct experience and mainly come in the form of nouns. It is later that verbs, adjectives and adverbs appear. With this in mind, it is easy to see what a rich opportunity the objects in the Treasure Basket can offer.

### Links to the Early Years Foundation Stage (practice guidance)

#### *Personal, Social and Emotional Development*

*Dispositions and attitudes*

- Have a strong exploratory impulse.
- Discover more about what they like and dislike.
- Learn that experiences can be shared.

#### *Communication, Language and Literacy*

*Language for thinking*

- Are intrigued by novelty and events and actions around them.

*Writing*

- Move arms and legs and increasingly use them to reach for, grasp and manipulate things.

#### *Problem Solving, Reasoning and Numeracy*

*Numbers as labels and for counting*

- Respond to people and objects in their environment.
- Notice changes in groupings of objects, images or sounds.

*Calculating*

- Are logical thinkers from birth.
- Are alert to and investigate things that challenge their expectations.

*Shape, space and measures*

- Develop an awareness of shape, form and texture as they encounter people and things in their environment.
- Find out what toys are like and can do through handling objects.

### Knowledge and Understanding of the World

*Exploration and investigation*

- Use movement and senses to focus on, reach for and handle objects.
- Learn by observation about actions and their effects.

*Designing and making*

- Explore objects and materials with hands and mouth.

### Physical Development

*Movement and space*

- Use movement and sensory exploration to link up with their immediate environment.

*Using equipment and materials*

- Reach out for, touch and begin to hold objects.

### Creative Development

*Being creative: responding to experiences, expressing and communicating ideas*

- Use movement and sensory exploration to connect with their immediate environment.
- Respond to what they see, hear, smell, touch and feel.

*Developing imagination and imaginative play*

- Smile with pleasure at recognisable playthings.
- Enjoy making noises or movements spontaneously.

# CHAPTER 5

# Offering the Treasure Basket

## How to create a Treasure Basket

The Treasure Basket comprises a suitable basket and a collection of between 80 and 100 different objects to put in the Basket. It is not a static piece of play material, as objects may be replaced (when worn or broken) and the collection can continue to grow over time. Every collection will be unique. The collection of objects in my own Treasure Basket was started nearly 30 years ago and has not only been a source of pleasure to many babies, it has also become, for me, a catalogue of memories and generosity.

Here are some guidelines when purchasing a Treasure Basket. The Basket should:

- be round in shape
- be made of wicker or some other natural material, which has no 'sharp bits'
- have rigid sides
- be 30 centimetres in diameter (internal measurement)
- be 12 centimetres in height
- be flat bottomed and have no handles.

(Treasure Baskets can be made to order from P.H. Coate and Son, www. coates–willowbasket.co.uk)

*Figure 5.1* The Treasure Basket contains 80–100 different household and natural objects, which are safe but small enough for a baby to pick up and handle

## Making the collection of objects

It is often said that the most difficult part of introducing the Treasure Basket into a nursery setting or your home is making the actual collection of objects. So why should it be so difficult?

What seems to happen is that, after the initial enthusiasm about the 'idea' of searching for objects, the pressing demands of childcare itself get in the way of giving time to going to the shops, searching your home or asking friends and family to find appropriate materials. While one can browse through an 'educational catalogue' during a break at lunchtime, making the time to visit kitchen shops and charity shops requires planning, organisation and co-operation with other colleagues.

What is more, there is often the disappointment of finding perhaps only half a dozen or so appropriate materials after an exhausting shopping expedition, with a daunting 80 more objects to collect. There have been many people who have given up collecting after about 20 objects, but then feel dissatisfied with the end result. The babies' interests have not been sustained and the rather empty-looking Treasure Basket is then only occasionally used.

However, this not need be the case, because with commitment and perseverance and 'with a little help from your friends', creating the Treasure Basket can become one of the most satisfying and creative things you may ever do, with regard to play materials. Indeed, it is an ongoing process as there are always more objects that could be added.

Here are some tips to get you started. If you want to create a really stimulating Treasure Basket, you will need to pursue the following strategy.

- Buy a suitable basket in which to place the objects (see previous section).

- Get parents and colleagues interested, so this exercise becomes a group project.

- Make a list of objects that you want to buy or look out for.

- Plan which shops to visit.

- Arrange a time, which is the least disruptive to your care setting, to make a shopping trip, preferably with another colleague. (It may involve a few shopping trips.)

- Enlist the help of parents to bring in suitable objects from home. (Make a suggestion list, to which parents can refer for guidance.)

- Look around your own home and ask relatives and friends to do the same. (Often the most interesting objects are those hidden away in drawers.)

- Collect objects from the countryside or seashore or ask others to do so for you.

- Visit your local 'resource centre', where you may find interesting and safe objects among the scrap materials on offer.

- Visit car boot sales, jumble sales and street markets.

- Be patient, resourceful and vigilant.

You will be richly rewarded for your efforts if you stick at this task, even if it takes a surprising number of months to create a stimulating collection of about 80 or so objects. What you will find is that, whenever or wherever you are shopping, you will find yourself looking at moderately small objects with new eyes.

*Figure 5.2* Collect objects of different colour, texture, taste, smell, weight and temperature. They can be made of metal, wood, leather, rubber, raffia and bristle, as well as natural objects

## Some ideas for Treasure Basket objects

*Natural objects*
- Shells (various types)
- Pine cone
- Loofah
- Large pebbles (various shapes)
- Pumice stone
- Sheepskin (10 × 5 cm)
- Grass rope
- Coconut shell
- A lemon
- An orange
- Sponge
- Avocado pear stone
- Piece of fur (10 × 5 cm)
- Piece of driftwood
- Gourd

*Objects made from wood*
- Curtain ring
- Spoons (various)
- Coaster
- Door wedge
- Block
- Bracelet
- Napkin ring
- Egg cup
- Ball
- Dowel
- Light pull
- Dolly peg
- Empty salt or pepper cellar
- Small turned bowl
- Spatula

*Objects made from metal*
- Bunch of keys
- Bangle

- Egg cup
- Buckle
- Curtain ring
- Napkin ring
- Egg poacher
- Drawer handle
- Spoons (various)
- Tea strainer/sieve
- Whisk
- Powder compact
- Plug and chain
- Silver ashtray
- Ornament
- Heavy chain
- Nutcracker
- Lid
- Small bowl
- Candle holder
- Lemon squeezer
- Key rings linked (10)
- Bell
- Set of measuring spoons on ring
- Ornament
- Chime bell
- Reindeer bells

### Objects made from leather and textile
- Leather wallet/purse/spectacle case
- Fabric wallet/purse/spectacle case
- Coloured ribbons
- Leather key ring
- Bag of herbs
- Lavender bag
- Velvet powder puff
- Piece of flannel and other fabric off-cuts (12 × 8 cm)
- Bean bag
- Juggling ball
- Small teddy bear

*Objects made from rubber*
- Ball
- Large eraser
- Coaster
- Soap holder
- Door stop

*Objects with bristles*
- Paintbrush
- Pastry brush
- Bottle brush (various sizes)
- Shaving brush
- Toothbrush
- Small shoe brush
- Nailbrush
- Make-up brush

*Objects made from glass and marble*
- Egg
- Incense stick holder
- Ornament
- Vanilla essence bottle
- Lid (e.g. decanter)
- Place name holder
- Small mirror (for make-up)

*Objects made from other materials*
- Hair roller
- Woollen ball
- Golf ball
- Cane bag handle
- Raffia mat
- Small ceramic pot
- Champagne cork
- Small basket
- Large button (5 cm)
- Scourer

## Management and storage of the objects

The Treasure Basket itself is not only an excellent container when presenting the collection of objects to a baby, it is also an ideal method of storage as well. However, it is advisable to cover the basket with a cloth if it is to be stored on an open shelf (rather than in a cupboard) to keep the objects dust-free.

When making the collection of objects, it is important to check that each object is in top-quality condition, especially as the recycled or natural objects will be unique, with the possibility of imperfections, such as sharp edges, loose fragments, etc. Newly manufactured objects should be perfectly safe, but they need to be checked, nevertheless, and cleaned before use. Indeed, all objects should be cleaned before they are placed in the Treasure Basket.

When objects begin to get tired (for example, the bristles of a brush are beginning to come loose or a sponge is flattened) or broken, then they should be removed and replacements provided. In this way the collection of objects will always be safe, as well as attractive, for exploration.

## Keeping the objects clean

The issue of keeping the objects clean can be a thorny one. When a baby has reached the stage of picking up and mouthing objects, then the need for sterilising everything is greatly reduced. One can no longer monitor everything that finds its way into a baby's mouth. It is amazing how a baby will manage to reach and find small objects under a sofa or rug or in the grass or on the patio (even when one feels that the baby has been safely placed on a clean rug out of reach of these areas). While it is agreed that materials need to be thoroughly cleaned and well-maintained, there can be a conflict of interests over the use of chemicals in the cleaning process.

Many caregivers soak the objects in a sterilising solution either daily or weekly. Others wipe the objects with disinfectant wipes or use disinfectant sprays to keep the materials clean. Some of the fabric-type materials are washed in a washing machine, while other objects are cleaned in a dishwasher. There are also caregivers who prefer to use simple washing-up liquid in a bowl of hot water and wash the objects by hand.

All these methods will do the job of keeping play materials clean and it is essential that materials are regularly cleaned to keep them fresh as well as in good condition.

Some natural materials may begin to disintegrate after repeated washing, so replacements need to be found when this happens.

## The impact of sterilisation on children's health

There is currently nationwide concern over the 'explosion' in numbers of very young children experiencing allergies (particularly in the past ten years). These can range from nut and other food allergies, skin allergies (such as eczema) and allergies causing breathing difficulties (such as asthma). While it was originally thought that the allergies were triggered by pollution, such as car exhausts with fumes being expelled at 'buggy height', medical experts are now putting forward very different theories. The impact of pollution on health is still being researched, but scientific evidence is now revealing that allergies and even certain life-threatening illnesses, like some childhood leukaemias, could be triggered by the 'over-sterile' environments of very young children.

It would appear that the development of babies' and young children's natural immune systems are being disrupted by lack of exposure to common germs. The dramatic increase in the use of disinfectant chemicals in cleaning products around the home and workplace and the parallel increase in allergies is no coincidence.

If there is an infection among the children, it is, of course, essential that the play material should be disinfected. However, certain research evidence opens up the debate about the extent to which one should be using strong chemicals to clean play materials.

I would go further and wish to consider the impact of young children ingesting these chemicals on a regular basis. Never before has a generation of very young children been so regularly exposed to such toxic material and so the long-term effects on health and development are as yet unknown. I would suggest that play materials are always *rinsed* in clean water after any type of cleaning product is used, whether it is washing–up liquid or a disinfectant cleaning product.

## Case study: pause for thought

Jenny is a conscientious and enthusiastic nursery worker in a large day care nursery in a rural setting. There are many animals in the nursery, both in the grounds and inside the building. Each of the playrooms also has an aquarium with goldfish for everyone to enjoy.

Jenny likes everything to be organised, tidy and clean. She admits to being almost obsessively clean and uses a disinfectant spray on most of the surfaces, including door handles, windowsills, tabletops and toys.

However, she noticed that the goldfish in the aquarium in her room were regularly dying and being replaced, unlike the thriving specimens in the other rooms, which were simply growing bigger.

It was only when a colleague pointed out that fish are sensitive to chemicals, that she made the connection between her use of the cleaning spray and the goldfish deaths. This then led to some discussion in the nursery about the possible effect that such sprays might be having on the children and a new policy for cleaning was established, promoting the use of less toxic material.

Jenny's fish are now thriving as well!

## What the Treasure Basket offers the baby

### Freedom and independence

The Treasure Basket offers a young baby the first taste of freedom and independence. In any culture, one is bound by rules and rituals and mutual interdependence. That is the basis of society, where groups can live and work together in reasonable harmony.

However, we all need to have a sense of our own uniqueness to feel fully human. We need to appreciate that we do have free will and can make choices, otherwise our spirit is stifled or turns negative.

In the earliest years of life, babies and young children need to feel they have freedom and independence to spread out and gather in, to explore and reflect. Young children need to be listened to and heard, to ask questions and be given answers. Indeed, we all need to be given the freedom that comes from being trusted and accepted, if we are to be able to take on the responsibility of the independence we seek, to use it positively for others as well as ourselves.

In being offered such a large collection of objects which are 'accessible', the baby is free to choose what he plays with without the need for permission or assistance. The choice is there for the baby to independently select *what* he wants to play with, *how* he wants to explore it and for *how long* he wants to play with it.

## Courage

Reaching out into the unknown requires courage. When a baby is seated beside a Treasure Basket for the fist time, he will always experience this subtle balance between anxiety and curiosity. Depending on the baby's personality, he will either take an immediate 'plunge' and grab at whatever objects are within easy reach, or he will look at them carefully or tentatively allow his hand to hover and lightly touch things.

However the baby approaches the objects, which are unfamiliar to him, it will take courage to touch and explore them. The Treasure Basket promotes the capacity for courage and the need to take risks in order to learn.

## Concentration

As the collection of objects in a Treasure Basket is so varied and numerous, a baby's interest is inevitably captured. Playing, he becomes totally absorbed in the sensory experiences which the objects provide. This focused and intense interest without distraction, the giving of all one's energies to a single purpose, is concentration.

The ability to concentrate is the fundamental skill required in all learning. The Treasure Basket facilitates concentration in babies of between 40 minutes to one hour. Regular experience of this level of concentration is probably the single most important skill that the Treasure Basket promotes.

## Setting up a session with the Treasure Basket

### When

As it is so easy to set up a session, there can be a fair measure of flexibility about the timing to suit the babies' needs and routines as well as the caregivers'. It is important, first of all, to check that the babies are physically comfortable (having been fed and wearing clean nappies and suitable clothing).

It is also important to choose a time of day when the babies are alert and refreshed. If they have recently been brought into the care setting then they need to be settled first, so they are emotionally calm and content.

The final point about the timing of a session is that it must be at a time when between half an hour and an hour can be set aside with the minimum of disruption. This is to avoid the distracting 'coming and going' and 'noise' of babies, their parents and caregivers.

*Figure 5.3* The attentive caregiver provides an atmosphere of safety and trust so the baby feels confident to explore the objects in the Treasure Basket

### How long

Ideally, it is good to offer a session lasting between 40 minutes and one hour. However, even a short session of 15 minutes will have plenty of 'play value' and takes very little time or effort to arrange.

### Where

You should find a quiet area, which is not part of a thoroughfare with people walking about. It needs to be a space where there is a comfortable soft-furnished chair for the adult and carpeted floor for the babies to sit on. It is a good idea to provide supporting cushions for the babies so they feel secure as they reach into the basket for objects. The carpeted space does not need to be more than two square metres in size.

However, it is important that this space is protected from the intrusion of toddlers or older children, who may inadvertently tread on the babies or be tempted to 'borrow' some of the objects.

### How often

Ideally, the Treasure Basket should be offered to the babies on a daily basis. However, as it is so important for the atmosphere to be calm and the caregiver quiet and attentive, it is better to miss a day if there is unexpected disruption or changes to routine (which create uncertainties for the babies).

## The contribution of the attentive adult

Since writing the first edition of this book, many practitioners have expressed their concern to me that, with the advent of the EYFS and the associated inspection process, colleagues have become more intrusive and directive than ever in the way they support young children in their play. There is increasing 'uneasiness' about sitting quietly, as it can be mistaken for 'just sitting there' and 'doing nothing'. It is therefore very important to understand 'how' the caregiver supports play and learning without taking over.

### Being an attentive facilitator

Facilitation is, by definition, an 'easing of the way'. The caregiver is not teaching the baby about the physical characteristics of objects or how to concentrate. By being attentive to the baby's emotions and intentions, the caregiver is supportive, responsive and unobtrusive so the baby is freely motivated to learn these things for himself. This might involve accepting the baby's offer of an object to you, exchanging a smile or gently retrieving an object that has rolled out of the baby's reach. One needs to develop the art of 'alert stillness', which means being observant and attentive without intrusion or distraction.

### Providing an atmosphere of trust

It is important that the caregiver has a secure and positive relationship with the baby, so the baby has a secure base from which to reach out, explore and enjoy the objects, knowing and trusting that the adult will be there to keep him safe.

### Management of one's own, and others', anxieties

As has been discussed in Chapter 4, it is important to be aware of one's own feelings about the objects that are offered, as negative feelings are communicated to the babies. Similarly, in order to promote trust between parents and paid caregivers, the caregivers need to be sensitive to parents' feelings and clearly explain the principles of the Treasure Basket, so there can be positive collaboration in the approach.

## Management of materials

It is the responsibility of the caregivers to make the collection of suitable and varied objects and to make sure they are in cleaned and replaced (when necessary) to keep them in top-quality condition.

Much emphasis is placed on the importance of adult–child interaction in the early years. One tends to think of this as involving the adult 'talking' to the child. While this is certainly the case for much of the time, it is not so at the Treasure Basket. The interaction is more subtle (than talking), as has been described in the previous paragraph. However, it is important that the caregiver does not carry out a conversation with another adult at this time, because the required attentiveness will be all but lost.

## The importance of sitting comfortably

Unless the adult is comfortable she will not be in the relaxed and alert state to be fully attentive. In addition, if the adult is not comfortable, the babies will not be really relaxed or comfortable either.

So what do I mean by being comfortable? Earlier in the book I have discussed the importance of being 'emotionally comfortable' with the materials on offer. However, it is equally important to feel physically comfortable too.

This means having a comfortable chair to sit on. Some people subscribe to the fallacy that being comfortable suggests that you are not alert in your work. This is *not* the case. Unless you can relax in an upholstered chair (or large bean bag) which supports your back, you will either find yourself noticing and being distracted by your physical discomfort or you will be moving about to alleviate it (and causing a disturbance) or missing something in the children's play. In the long run, you are storing up back problems for yourself. Your comfort is an essential part of a successful Treasure Basket session.

# CHAPTER 6

# Heuristic Play

## 'What can I do with the object?'

### When does this play begin?

Usually the age at which children can be observed to embark on Heuristic Play is around nine to ten months, although this chronological age can vary according to the individual child's rate of development. However, one can say that it starts when a baby begins to move about and show interest in what he can do with things. Essentially, he discovers that, not only can he move his own body about, but he can also move objects from one place to another as well.

This type of play then continues to predominate until it becomes less about scientific experimentation and more about domestic and social re-enactment, as the toddler's interest in and use of expressive language begins to increase (at around two years of age).

In one sense, any form of scientific enquiry could be described as Heuristic Play, and it continues throughout life for those seeking to understand and to make better sense of the physical world.

### What the term 'Heuristic Play' means

Heuristic Play comes from the Greek word 'eurisko', which means 'I find' or 'I discover'. It is derived from the ancient tale about Archimedes, who was supposed to have discovered the law of the displacement of water when he got into the bath and saw that his own body caused the level of water in the bath to rise. He leapt out of the bath, jumping with joy and shouting, 'Eureka!' ('I have discovered – I now understand!').

This is precisely the experience a toddler has when he puts an object inside a container and discovers, to his delight, that a smaller object will fit inside a hollow larger object, or that flat surfaced objects can be piled up, or that round objects can be rolled.

From a toddler's point of view, 'What can I do with it?' becomes his primary interest in relation to handling objects. It is for this reason that small objects will be 'posted' into any available containing space.

## Examples of 'discovered posting places' for small objects

Nursery staff are often bemused or amused at the way toys and other small objects seem to disappear in a playroom. These are some common places where these things have been placed:

- through the holes around the hollow legs of some raised sandpits;
- inside the protective cover surrounding a stair-gate hinge;
- through the protective grill covering a radiator or other heating device;
- inside rubbish bins and laundry baskets;
- under the cushions of soft chairs or sofas;
- inside the slot for the tape in a video recorder;
- down the toilet;
- under the lowest bookshelf of a bookcase;
- in large pockets of the toddlers' own clothes.

It is therefore of vital importance to provide appropriate materials to children at this stage to stimulate and satisfy their curiosity. Otherwise the caregivers will either have to cope with frustrated children throwing objects about or waste time extracting awkwardly placed objects from inappropriate corners of the playroom.

## What toys are normally on offer to the toddler

In terms of the play experiences that are offered to children of this age, there is usually a lot of variety. This may range from clambering on foam blocks, playing with sand, water and paint, as well as other sensory material (such as dried pasta or dough), to the social play of songs, rhymes and looking at books. Those toddlers with the benefit of a garden, park or natural habitat will have the added experience of playing in puddles or with leaves or finding small stones, beetles or insects.

However, when it comes to the actual toys that are normally on offer to a toddler, then the picture becomes deceptively sterile. Most of the manufactured toys which are provided for this age group are made of plastic and are very expensive. While they are often attractively complicated and 'educational' from an adult perspective, they are woefully limited in their potential for discovery from the toddler's point of view. This is because many of the manufactured toys have 'correct' or 'single' response features and do not allow for the real discovery of new concepts through the child's own activity. Also, many of the manufactured toys are far too difficult for children of this age and so they will quickly lose interest in them.

For example, a classic toy that can be purchased is the 'shape sorter' or 'posting box'. While, in principle, this kind of toy will satisfy the desire of a toddler to 'put an object into a hollow space', the shapes of the objects and matching spaces are, in many cases, becoming ridiculously complicated. There are now shape sorters where the objects are shaped as letters or numbers. This is absurd, as the toddler has no notion yet of the concept of numbers or letters, let alone the ability to recognise that shapes represent these things. What is even more significant is that these shapes are much too intricate for children of this age to put the right shape through the right hole successfully. What is more likely to happen is that these shapes will find themselves 'posted' in other places, (such as those already mentioned) or the whole toy will be discarded.

Recently, there was a version of the 'letter and number' type of shape sorter which had rubber shapes and it was found that children were able to squash the shapes into 'incorrect' holes. Instead of recognising the ingenuity of the children when faced with the meaningless of the actual shapes, the manufacturers have now reverted to rigid plastic shapes of letters and numbers and nursery workers have noticed that this toy has now lost its play appeal.

Other toys, which have a single or correct way of playing with them, are those such as graded stacking rings, simple inset puzzles and push-button toys (where a single picture pops up or a noise is produced). Although all play materials will arouse curiosity initially, they will either soon be discarded (such as the push-button toys) or the 'pieces', like the rings or puzzle shapes, will find their way into other places.

One must also beware of the educational claims of such manufactured toys. At worst, they are bogus and at best they can trigger anxiety in the caregiver if the child is not playing with the toy 'correctly' and so may be, from a skills-based educational point of view, failing.

### Case study: the story of the anxious mother, the shape sorter and the resourceful toddler

Sarah was the mother of 12-month-old Tom, a lively and happy toddler. She came to his nursery one day expressing her worries to the staff that her son might not be developing at the expected rate because he was not playing with one of his toys 'properly', even though he 'should' be able to, according to the age guidelines on the box.

The toy in question was a shape sorter (posting box) in the shape of a house. The roof acted as a lid and had a selection of shaped holes in it with the square block shape fitting in through the chimney. The main house part was the container for the shapes.

Most children under the age of two will repeat a sequence of actions over and over again in their play. Tom was no exception as he had a regular way of playing with this particular toy. He would lift the roof lid off, empty out all the shapes and replace the lid. He then selected the cylinder and the square block shapes and successfully 'posted' them through their holes. (These shapes are the simplest and therefore are appropriate for a child of this age.) He then lifted off the roof, put all the rest of the shapes in the box, replaced the roof and shook the whole house, before starting the sequence all over again.

Tom's mother was worried that he was not playing with the toy 'properly' as he was not posting the complex star, triangle, cross, etc. through their appropriately shaped holes. So she devised a plan. She used tape to stick the roof to the rest of the house so that Tom would have to play with the toy properly.

However, Tom had not reached the stage in his development where he would be able to orientate these shapes accurately. So when he picked up his familiar toy and saw the shapes loose outside, he posted the cylinder and block before trying, unsuccessfully, to take the roof off. Undaunted, he noticed the sticky tape, something he had never seen before, and was intrigued. For the next 15 minutes or so he examined this new material with such interest that he unwittingly managed to loosen the end of the tape. Much to his mother's astonishment he then unravelled the tape with deep concentration and interest, discovering this long stuff was sticky and got longer and longer! Eventually he managed to take the whole length of tape off and proceeded to lift the roof off his shape sorter with a look of both triumph and delight, before continuing his normal game.

The nursery staff helped Tom's mother to see that, in fact, he had been playing with curiosity and concentration and had used the novelty of the sticky tape to extend his play into a whole new area of discovery. The complex shapes were inappropriate for Tom but, instead of feeling defeated, frustrated or a failure, he simply found an alternative way to achieve what he had set out to do and to derive satisfaction in his play. This is the underlying principle of Heuristic Play.

## There is no failure with Heuristic Play

The very fact that a toddler is seeking to find out what he can do with objects and then moves them about, places them in containers and piles them up, etc., implies there is no failure. For example, if a toddler were to drop a ping-pong ball through a tube, the ball would shoot out of the other end and bounce on the floor. He is then likely to repeat this action with tremendous delight. If he then were to pick up a tennis ball, he would discover that it would not fit in the tube (the ball is too big). On the other hand, if he picked up a small brick, he might discover that, although it will fit through the tube, it lands with a plop rather than a bounce (square things do not bounce). Using a discarded cardboard tube (such as that used for wrapping paper) and different objects, he is discovering many new concepts, as well as discovering different outcomes to his experimentation.

Different outcomes stimulate thinking and greater understanding about the nature of different materials. A greater understanding is immensely satisfying and motivating. So, failing to get a brick to bounce or a large ball to pass down a small tube does not imply failure to the toddler.

The idea of 'failure' or 'not doing something properly' is an idea conjured up by the adults and not by the children.

## What toddlers 'do' that makes it Heuristic Play

A toddler wants to make things happen. He develops an interest in causality, the cause-and-effect relationships between objects. He wants to explore the effect of his action upon objects. To begin with, things seem random and in chaos. However, it is out of the chaos and the endless possibilities that patterns and order emerge.

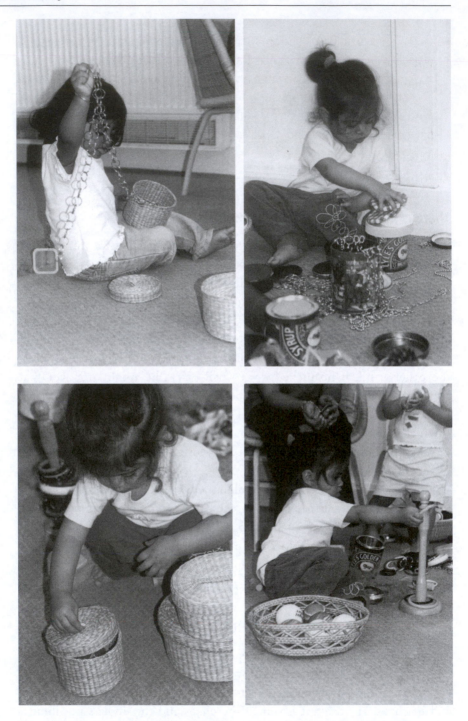

*Figure 6.1* Heuristic Play: a time of activity, purpose and intense concentration

At first, toddlers have a preoccupation with what they can do with their bodies, so they show interest in doing things like climbing up stairs and onto furniture, or crawling under tables or behind curtains. They seek adult responses for this kind of behaviour, partly to ensure their safety (by your vigilance) and partly to share in their sheer delight of their physical achievement and sense of daring and adventure.

Alongside the interest in what they can do with their bodies is the interest in what they can do with objects. Below is a typical set of behaviours, which describe Heuristic Play:

- pick up objects, move them about and put them in different places;
- put objects into containers, such as tins, boxes, purses, tubes and pull-along trolleys;
- take objects out of containers and place them elsewhere;
- pile objects on top of one another and then knock the pile down;
- pour objects (or water) from one container into another;
- roll objects along the floor;
- slide objects through sloping tubes or down sloping surfaces;
- slot small objects inside larger objects;
- shake or bang objects together or use their hands to bang objects;
- line objects up;
- collect similar or same objects, usually putting them in a container;
- put rings on rods, posts, handlebars, etc.;
- spin cylindrical or round-shaped objects;
- drop objects from a height;
- screw and unscrew lids;
- stick and detach Velcro hair rollers, constructional material, etc.;
- squeeze objects in fists or between forefingers and thumb;
- look inside or through objects;
- drape things, like ribbons, chains or scarves around their necks;
- push one object into a new place with another object.

## New concepts learnt through Heuristic Play

When young children in the second year of life are busy with the concentrated activity of filling and emptying, piling, sorting, etc., it is easy to observe the behaviour and see it simply in terms of physical or motor coordination skills only. However, while these obvious physical skills are of paramount importance, it is the underlying concepts being developed which are creating the foundations of abstract thought.

## Abstract thought

Abstract thought is the ability to think about and interpret information in one's imagination without the concrete material being there. To understand the concept of size, for example, you need to have 'an idea of largeness and smallness'. It is useful to have a concept of size for all mathematical and scientific thinking, whether it is about planning to cook a meal for a specific number of people or working out how much paint is needed to paint a room. One needs to be able to *think* about these things *before* the action can be competently and efficiently carried out.

So much of our daily activity in adulthood relies on understanding and being able to use a range of abstract concepts, yet we are barely aware of this. The ability to work with numbers and scientific laws underpins much of the curriculum in schools from the age of four right up to the leaving age of 16 and beyond.

However, one needs to 'play around' with the concrete materials (objects) in order to understand and develop the concepts, which can then be applied in all sorts of different situations. Once you have an understanding of size (for example, through having discovered through play that small things fit into big things, but not the other way round and that some things are the same size but they do not fit inside each other), then these concepts can be applied to anything.

So this begs the question of what kind of concepts does the toddler begin to learn through all the experimental activity already identified? Even before a child has the language to describe or explain these concepts, he nevertheless has an understanding of them. When his language begins to develop, he will already have the understanding to back up the words he hears and uses. Typical concepts might include:

- same and different;
- round things roll;
- some round things bounce, but cylinders do not bounce;
- spheres roll in all directions;

- little fits inside big;
- little and big are different;
- some things with the same shape have different weights;
- some things are hollow and others are solid;
- some things are long and others are short;
- shiny reflects;
- metal resonates;
- absorbency of material (such as the difference between a sponge and a stone);
- flat objects can be piled up;
- one, a few and many;
- floating and sinking;
- heavy and light.

Indeed, the list of basic scientific and mathematical concepts could be extended even further, and the reader may wish to do this. If one watches the activity of a toddler with objects, simple behaviour can be seen in a much more sophisticated light and can be a source of absorbing interest for the observant adult.

## Piaget's schemas

One of the greatest thinkers of the twentieth century was Jean Piaget. For over 80 years, his observations and theories of child development have shaped and influenced our understanding of how children learn. Piaget's genius lay in seeing a greater intelligence beyond a baby's or toddler's limited behaviours.

Piaget noticed that there seemed to be patterns of behaviour, which he described as 'schemas', that all children use in their play. He suggested that these behavioural schemas represent 'ways of thinking' that help children to classify their experiences in order to make sense of the world around them. The most common schemas are:

- **rotating** – a fascination with roundness and things being able to roll;
- **enveloping** – a fascination with wrapping and covering objects and themselves;

- **containing** – a fascination with filling and emptying containers;
- **connecting** – a fascination with fitting things together and joining themselves to things;
- **transporting** – a fascination with collecting and moving objects and themselves about.

All these schemas can be observed when a toddler is playing with Heuristic Play materials and become more complex and elaborate as children begin to use language and imagination.

## Developing the use of 'Learning Tools'

> Out of the baby's unspecific body activity, patterns begin to emerge. These patterns of behaviour are the Learning Tools, mental or cognitive tools used by all children, cross-culturally, to learn and solve problems. The tools are Placing, Piling, Banging, Pairing, Matching, Sorting, Sequencing and Brick Building. The development of early play and learning in the young child is a highly complex process. The Learning Tools are interrelated and interdependent; they are rarely seen in isolation. They are sometimes seen in parallel, sometimes they overlap, sometimes they seem to merge, but they are always identifiable in the early play and learning of the very young child.
>
> (Stroh *et al.* 2008: 13)

Katrin Stroh and Thelma Robinson base their therapeutic practice (Functional Learning) with developmentally delayed children on the earliest experiences of the normal child resulting in the development of what they call the 'Learning Tools'. They state that the fundamental Learning Tool is picking up and *placing*, which they define as filling a space with an object. We learn nothing about how we interact with the world unless we can intentionally pick something up and let it go or move it about from place to place.

The Learning Tools, which they identify as being the basis of all future problem-solving skills, are as follows:

- **placing** – filling a space with an object, which means moving it from one place to another.
- **banging** – when one object is banged against another. At first this is with one hand only, but later it involves the ability to use both hands together either to bring objects together (like banging together two bricks) or to bang two separate objects on a different object (like using

two sticks to bang a drum). This promotes rhythmic movement of the whole body and integrates the neural connections between both sides of the brain. Such activity eventually leads to the use of tools (of the utensil type) as an extension of the child's arm to 'make a mark on' and 'manipulate' the environment. The obvious step is the ability to express oneself through drawing and, later, writing.

- **pairing and matching** – is noticing that two things are the same and then choosing to bring them together. As a toddler discovers that different objects can be alike and begins to engage in pairing, this leads to the capacity for actively comparing and contrasting one pattern or object with another and deliberately holding one thing in mind as he searches for another identical or similar thing. As children begin to understand the function of different objects, this Learning Tool enables them to select and make choices, such as being able to find a cup or glass to drink out of, from a collection of plates, bowls, vases and other dishes.

- **sorting** – is a particular way of thinking which uses flexibility to sort out and make sense of the world by recognising that various objects are the same or similar and then classifying them. It is very important for children to develop the ability to sort out their world in order to feel safe, such as classifying people as family, friends and strangers or identifying that things with four legs and a seat are for sitting on.

- **piling** – is the deliberate placing of one object on top of another, like brick building, to produce or reproduce a model. This Learning Tool enables a child to develop the ability to have an idea in mind (a mental image) in order to create a structure and then to be able actually to build it.

- **sequencing** – Katrin Stroh has stated (in many personal conversations) that all the Learning Tools depend on the child's ability to continue his activities in an ongoing manner. In other words, this behaviour is the ability to carry out a series of activities in sequence. This sequencing activity allows the child to arrange and order things and to anticipate and predict what is to come and is the basis of logical verbal reasoning.

## How Heuristic Play is a 'non-social' activity and promotes concentration

Heuristic Play can be described as a 'non-social' activity because the activities and the acquisition of skills do not depend on direct interaction with another person. In particular, a toddler does not need verbal encouragement or praise to be motivated or excited by what he is doing. The activity itself is its own reward and the 'cause and effect' nature of Heuristic Play provides its own encouragement.

Although the presence of an attentive and caring adult is necessary (and will be discussed in the next chapter), the normal social rewards of verbal encouragement, clapping of hands and so on are not only unnecessary, they can be downright intrusive and disturbing.

It is easier to appreciate this idea if you consider an absorbing activity that you enjoy doing. This may be reading a book, doing a jigsaw puzzle, preparing a meal or finding something on the Internet. Imagine that another person came up to you and told you how well you were doing and started to give you advice or got very close to you. You would probably find yourself distracted, lose the thread of your thinking and become thoroughly disappointed and frustrated that your pleasure in being lost in thought had been broken.

This is precisely the experience of a toddler when he is engaged in Heuristic Play. Whereas a toddler is easily distracted and appeased by an adult (and would not hold the grudges that an adult might if we were interrupted) he will nevertheless have his pleasure in deep concentration broken. Part of the satisfaction of Heuristic Play is that it offers the opportunity for deep and sustained concentration.

When teachers express concern about the learning difficulties of children with special educational needs, they are usually referring to difficulties with concentration and sustained activity. Sadly, many children lose their inborn ability to concentrate and be still with a focus of interest. Bettelheim (1987) described this as 'stick-to-itiveness' and it is a word, which precisely describes the experience afforded by Heuristic Play.

### Links to the Early Years Foundation Stage (practice guidance)

#### *Personal, Social and Emotional Development*

*Dispositions and attitudes*

- Explore the environment with interest.
- Discover more about what they like and dislike.
- Develop a curiosity about things and processes.
- Take pleasure in learning new skills.

*Self-confidence and self-esteem*

- Make choices that involve challenge, when adults ensure their safety.

- Explore from the security of a close relationship with a caring and responsive adult.

- Develop confidence in own abilities.

## Communication, Language and Literacy

*Language for thinking*

- Are intrigued by novelty and events and actions around them.

## Problem Solving, Reasoning and Numeracy

*Numbers as labels and for counting*

- Distinguish between quantities, recognising that a group of objects is more than one.

*Calculating*

- Are learning to classify by organising and arranging toys with increasing intent.

- Are alert to and investigate things that challenge their expectations.

*Shape, space and measures*

- Recognise big things and small things in meaningful contexts.

- Find out what toys are like and can do through handling objects.

- Use blocks to create their own simple structures and arrangements.

- Enjoy filling and emptying containers.

## Knowledge and Understanding of the World

*Exploration and investigation*

- Sometimes focus their enquiries on particular features or processes.

*Designing and making*

- Show curiosity and interest in things that are built up and fall down, and that open and close.
- Are interested in pushing and pulling things, and begin to make structures.

### Physical Development

*Using equipment and materials*

- Become absorbed in putting objects in and out of containers.
- Begin to make, and manipulate, objects and tools.
- Put together a sequence of actions.

### Creative Development

*Being creative: responding to experiences,
expressing and communicating ideas*

- Explore by repeating patterns of play.
- Respond to what they see, hear, smell, touch and feel.

# CHAPTER 7

# Offering Heuristic Play material

## Making the collection of materials

Probably the very first thing, when making the collection of materials, is to buy or make 15 large fabric drawstring bags (in the style of the old-fashioned shoe bag). These bags will then serve to contain 15 individual collections of objects, neatly and safely. If you manage to collect more than 15 types of object, then obviously you will need a corresponding number of bags. The next step is to make the collections of objects and containers.

## *The objects*

For the Heuristic Play collection there should be about 50 examples of each chosen object for a group of six toddlers. This means that you will need to provide, for example, 50 hair rollers, 50 pine cones, 50 pom-poms, 50 coloured ribbons and so on. If you are working in a situation where there are never more than two toddlers together then, of course, you will not need to have so many of each item.

The objects will be drawn from many different sources:

- **natural** objects (pebbles, shells, etc.);
- **household** objects (rubber door wedges, wooden doorknobs, wooden dolly pegs, etc.);
- **recycled** objects (metal lids, corks, cardboard tubes, etc.);
- **toys** (rubber balls, wheeled wooden vehicles, wooden bricks, etc.); and
- **general purpose** objects (bath chains, hair rollers, coasters, scourers, etc.).

Indeed, the possibilities for safe but interesting objects become endless, once you begin to look out for them.

### The containers

The collection of objects will have limited play value unless there is also a good and extensive range of containers. As has already been explained, the toddler wants to move things about and put things into and take them out of containers. Probably the two most popular containers are metal tins and cardboard tubes (with or without 'ends'). Both these types of container are recycled items, so some thought must be given to determining how one goes about collecting them in sufficient numbers.

With regard to *tins*, there are many different types which can be used. Empty baby formula milk, coffee and syrup tins are ideal because they are a good size and have lift-off lids, leaving a safe rim. It is not safe to use tins which have a ring-pull opening or which require a tin opener, as the rims can be sharp.

Used biscuit tins, coffee and tea tins and whisky bottle tins are further examples of safe rimmed tins, which are readily available. However, there are plenty of other tins which can also be used.

Tubes are also readily available from items such as stacking crisps and various sweets, as well as those that can be obtained from the post office for sending rolled papers through the post. Open-ended tubes can be obtained from the inner tubes of, for example, kitchen towels, foil and wrapping paper, but there are plenty of others if one looks around. If the tubes from rolls of toilet paper are used, then they must be sterilised by placing them in a microwave oven for a few seconds.

Other useful containers are washed plastic jars, wide-necked bottles, yoghurt pots, flower pots, baskets of various sizes, small jars of thick glass and shoe boxes. Indeed, the range of possible containers is extensive and many are included in the section below where a suggested list is presented.

### Natural objects

If you are fortunate to live near the countryside or the sea, then you have the advantage of easily being able to find items such as pine cones, shells and pebbles in the local area. However, even if you live in a city, you can ask willing parents and colleagues to collect items for you when they go on holiday, or you may be able to do the same. You can often buy natural objects, such as bags of seashells, in shops selling sophisticated items as bathroom accessories or natural ornaments. Seasonal fruits like conkers may be found under horse chestnut trees in local parks or on roadsides. Some people are nervous about using conkers with children because of the concern about nut allergies. In my experience, conkers have been perfectly safe but you may want to check with parents, nursery managers or medical advisers before using them in your workplace.

### Household objects

The best shops to start with when looking for these kinds of objects are 'kitchenware' shops, department stores and ironmongers. Often objects (such as wooden doorknobs, pastry brushes and bunches of keys), which in the past have held little interest, become potentially coveted play materials.

### Recycled objects

One of the best features of Heuristic Play is that it is a genuinely environmentally friendly way of using material for children to develop their play. Indeed, it is often recycled material that offers the best potential for play, such as the used tubes and tins already mentioned, as well as items such as jar lids, cotton reels, electric cable spools, sheets of bubble wrap and empty crisp packets. Some objects may only have a 'one play session' value, such as a range of cardboard boxes, but others, like jar lids, may last for years.

It is a good idea to ask parents and colleagues for help and also to see what new ideas people have. Another way of acquiring recycled material is to visit your nearest resource centre, sometimes known as the 'scrap project', where office and light manufacturing recycled material can be obtained. Many of these centres offer generous concession rates to those working with young children, which can prove to be an economical way of purchasing interesting objects.

### Toys

There are various manufactured toys which are ideal in promoting Heuristic Play, such as wooden bricks or large-scale constructional toys. Wheeled wooden vehicles and pull–along toys (especially those which can carry things) will always be popular as they can be moved about so easily. Any kind of safe ball, such as foam balls, rubber balls, ping–pong balls and inflatable balls are all excellent. Simple stacking cubes can be enjoyed, whether they are stacked in size order or not. When selecting bought toys always have in mind the question, 'What different ways can the children use this toy?'

## *General purpose objects*

These objects can be purchased from a variety of shops, such as chemists for hair rollers, slotted boxes and coasters from department stores, bath chains from DIY stores, measuring spoons from kitchenware shops and ribbons from haberdashers. Other sources for objects can be car boot sales, markets, charity shops and so on.

### Suggested materials to promote Heuristic Play

*Containers*
- Biscuit or whisky tins with lids
- Various sized tins with smooth rims
- Wide-necked plastic bottles
- Yoghurt pots or jars
- Glass jars (tiny ones with thick glass)
- Flower pots
- Nesting Ali Baba baskets
- Cardboard or wooden boxes (with/without lids)
- Cardboard tubes (e.g. from sweets or stacking crisps)

*Objects to collect or make*
- Cardboard cylinders (e.g. insides of kitchen paper, cling film or foil)
- 1 metre lengths of silk or velvet ribbon or lace
- Sanded wooden off-cuts from a carpenter
- Bunches of keys
- Metal jar lids of all sizes (jam, pickle, coffee, etc.)
- Wine and champagne bottle corks (large)
- Pine cones and shells
- Very large buttons (5 cm diameter)
- Different sized metal or wooden spoons

*Objects to buy*
- Curtain rings (wooden and metal)
- Rubber door wedges
- Wooden dolly pegs (smooth)
- Lengths of bath chain (some 50 cm, some 1 metre)
- Key ring links (10 links make a long enough chain)
- Round wooden doorknobs

- Simple figures (without moving parts)
- Small wheeled wooden vehicles

## Objects which carry and contain
- Large measuring spoons
- Purses and wallets
- Baskets and rigid carrier bags
- Large water containers with handles
- Ice cube trays
- Cutlery drainers with holes
- Wooden mug trees

## Objects which stack
- Kitchen roll holders with bracelets and curtain rings
- Wooden bricks of various sizes
- Small boxes of various sizes
- Set of nesting coasters

## Objects which roll
- Pom-poms
- Hair rollers
- Rubber balls
- Ping-pong balls
- Wooden balls
- Foam balls
- Cotton reels
- Electrical cable spools (empty)
- Tubes (plastic or cardboard)

## Posting objects
- Shoes boxes with holes in lid and set of balls
- Boxes with slits in lid and large buttons (min. 5 cm diametre)
- Tins with holes in lid and drinking straws

## Slotting objects
- Rubber or wooden CD storage and square coasters or CDs
- Money boxes and large buttons
- Several cardboard or plastic tubes with slight differences in diameter
- Several hair rollers of different sizes

## Management and storage of the materials

The best way to store the collections of objects safely is to use drawstring bags, which can be hung from coat hooks on a spare portion of wall. The containers may need to be stacked and it is often useful to install a high shelf for this purpose.

It is extremely important that the material is kept in tip top condition as it needs to look attractive and be well cared for to reflect the importance placed on the provision of Heuristic Play. Some people imagine that the objects are used (and therefore dirty or damaged in some way) and this puts them off collecting such ordinary things. On the contrary, however, the manufactured objects need to be either new or 'as new' and, in the case of recycled or natural materials, cleaned and checked for any sharp edges and so on. Brushes with loose bristles, flattened tubes or shells with broken edges, for example, need to be removed and replaced.

## Keeping the materials clean

The ways in which the Heuristic Play materials are kept clean are identical to the methods employed for the Treasure Basket materials (see Chapter 5).

It is important that there is a clear policy in your place of work about the cleaning of play materials and that this is followed. Parents must feel happy and confident that their children are being provided with high-quality play material. The natural, household and recycled objects are particularly vulnerable to appearing inferior if they are not kept as clean as if they were new (or in the case of material such as the cardboard tubes, regularly replaced when damaged).

Some material will require more regular cleaning, but decisions about this must be at the discretion of your manager, health and safety adviser and parents.

## How to set up a Heuristic Play session

### When

The very first thing to consider when setting up a Heuristic Play session is to choose a period of time in the children's day when they are neither tired nor hungry and when there is likely to be no disruption. It cannot be stated clearly enough that this play is best facilitated when the children are able to concentrate on their play without interference or interruption.

Many caregivers find that late morning or after the afternoon sleep seem to be the optimum periods of the day in a nursery setting, when the children have all arrived and when all the staff are on duty. In a private home or during a mother and toddler session, the times may be quite different.

*Figure 7.1* The objects are attractively set out at the beginning of a Heuristic Play session

### How long

It would appear that an hour is the best length of time to allow for the session but, in many nursery settings it is almost impossible to secure a whole hour without interruption.

However, one needs enough time to prepare the space, to allow the children their play and to clear up. It is best if an adult can put out the play materials without the children around her feet. The children can then come into an inviting space with all the materials attractively laid out.

It is important that, however long the session lasts, there should be 15 to 20 minutes allowed (within the session time) for the clearing up process with the assistance of the children.

### Where

A cleared space within the playroom or another small 'quiet' room is ideal. The space needs to be clearly defined, either by the use of a carpet on the floor or furnishings, such as cupboards or a sofa, to mark the boundaries. The benefit of using a carpet is that it helps to keep the atmosphere calm and quiet.

The space needs to be large enough for the group of children to be able to move around safely without bumping into other children and select material easily.

Other toys and play material should be cleared away or covered up, so the children are able to focus entirely on the Heuristic Play objects and containers.

### How often

As this play is so vital to a toddler's development, I would recommend that it should be offered on a daily basis (though once a day is sufficient). However, I do recognise that this can prove to be impossible in some cases, with all the other demands in a day care environment. In the home setting, it should prove very easy to provide every day.

For this play to be really beneficial, though, it should be offered two to three times a week and the collection of materials varied on each occasion.

### How much material

Ideally, there should be three tins and three tubes per child for each session. Further containers are also good, although you do not necessarily have to provide three of each for every child. You may decide to put out something like six bottles, ten flowerpots and only two boxes, for example, and this would be fine.

It is a good idea to put out the objects from about five of the bags at any one time and to change the combination of objects at each session. It then becomes very interesting to see how children use different combinations in different ways and whether, on one day, certain objects capture their interest more than on another day.

The material can be attractively set out within the play area in any way that looks appealing to you, as it will then appeal to the children.

### Clearing up

It is good to start clearing up about 15 minutes before the end of the session, so the unhurried atmosphere can continue to the very end.

For this process, it is really good to involve the children. As they love to fill and empty and sort, the clearing up simply becomes an adult-directed form of filling and sorting for them and so they love to do it. The adult has the bags ready and invites the children to select the materials and bring them to her to place in the bag.

The drawstring has the advantage of allowing the adult to quickly close the bag so objects cannot be taken out again, as well as stopping objects from getting into the wrong bags.

*Figure* 7.2 The caregiver is gentle and responsive towards the toddler's show of curiosity and interest during a Heuristic Play session

During this part of the session the adult can freely use language to give direction, offer encouragement and share pleasure in the process, so this becomes a sociable activity for the children.

## The contribution of the attentive adult

If someone who is unfamiliar with the principles of Heuristic Play were to walk in on a session, that person could well mistakenly assume that the adult supervising the session is doing nothing. At first glance it might appear that way.

However, as with the Treasure Basket, the role of the adult is to be attentive, responsive and unobtrusive in order to facilitate a feeling of safety, free choice of activity and high levels of concentration in the children.

There are some subtle differences, though, in the contribution of the attentive adult with the toddler engaging in Heuristic Play in comparison with the baby playing with a Treasure Basket.

Here are some of the main contributions that the adult makes:

- As toddlers can move about, there is a much greater risk of two children wanting the same object or container at the same time. This is where the abundance of material is so important, as the adult can discreetly lean forward and offer the second child another tube, chain, tin, etc. This is usually accepted with barely a glance and both children can continue their play in harmony. Children of this age have no understanding of sharing and it creates an emotionally stressful situation if the adult intervenes and tries to make them share. The only other option is to offer something completely different as a distraction.

    Although toddlers are unable to share (in the sense of taking turns with the use of something), they are often very curious about what other children are doing and you will often find that they copy one another's play behaviour. Building towers or making a loud noise by banging objects are common ways in which children of this age enjoy copying one another.

- Another common situation occurs when a child may be struggling with an impossible task that he has set himself, like trying to push a ball which is too large down a tube. This is an opportunity for the adult, once again, to discreetly offer a smaller ball for the child to try. If the child refuses or shows no interest, that is absolutely fine as it is the child's choice. However, he may accept the offer of the smaller ball and this will facilitate further satisfying play with those two items.

- There can be times when a child hurts himself or seeks out the adult for comfort or shared pleasure in something. This is when being attentive is so important because you are able quickly to respond to whatever is wanted and needed in a calm, reassuring and positive manner.

- Another task of the adult is to keep an eye on the steadily developing muddle of material as the session progresses, and do some unobtrusive reordering so that the children can more easily see what is available again and maybe have a new play idea.

- Essentially, as with the Treasure Basket, the adult needs to be still, quiet, attentive, gentle, responsive and comfortable.

## The importance of being comfortable

An essential part of setting up the Heuristic Play session is to provide the supervising adults with comfortable furniture to sit on. The importance of being comfortable has already been stressed in Chapter 5.

An upholstered chair, a sofa or large beanbag are all possible furnishings, which offer support for the back and are comfortable. Large cushions are also an option if you are able to support your back against a wall. (Few people can sit comfortably on the floor without back support for long.)

After 25 years or so of running workshops, I am still shocked to learn from those who attend that many nursery workers still do not have something comfortable to sit on. It would be wonderful if a comfortable chair was viewed as being as important a piece of furnishing for the room as a nappy changing table or a water tray.

## How to help colleagues and parents understand the approach

As some of the principles of Heuristic Play are unfamiliar to many parents and colleagues, it is important to make sure that you feel confident about sharing these principles in a way that inspires and enthuses them.

Some parents or colleagues (or, indeed, advisers and inspectors) might be anxious about the actual materials used, some might not be able to appreciate the play value because the children are not making anything 'concrete' with the materials. Some people may think that the children need active encouragement or praise and misinterpret the quiet attentiveness as lack of adult support.

So how can the message be communicated? These are some well-tried and effective ways of helping others to understand, be involved and support this play and learning:

- Invite parents to observe a Heuristic Play session.
- Show the parents a film about Heuristic Play, which can then be discussed afterwards (an example is *Heuristic Play with Objects* available from the National Children's Bureau).
- Give parents a list of all the materials used.
- Organise a meeting for parents where the principles can be explained, including the Learning Tools and suggested play material.
- Invite parents to collect objects and containers, so they can become involved in the process.

- Take photographs of the children at play so the parents can see what they are doing with the material.

- Share the children's learning through Heuristic Play with the parents, by reporting things they have done that day, either through a record book or by telling the parents directly when they come to pick up their child.

- Encourage the parents to make their own collections of objects and containers at home.

- Take any parental concerns seriously and be prepared to make time to talk them through. It is easy to overlook parental concern if you become very enthusiastic about something yourself. It is also easy to become defensive if you feel your professionalism is being challenged.

# CHAPTER 8

# Play with a purpose
# (two- to three-year-olds)

## 'What can this object become?'

### What is our purpose in life?

The main purpose that we all strive for throughout our lives is to find meaning. This comes from a deep spiritual impulse and is not about whether or not we have a religious faith. Meaning comes from 'understanding' and 'awareness'. When we feel that we have knowledge about something, and understand it better, then that enables us to predict and manipulate what might happen, which gives us a feeling of being confident, safe and in control.

Understanding is also about appreciation, because you can identify with what you understand and, by making it a part of you, you accept it. It may be that the reason you are reading this book is to give you a greater understanding about children's play and learning and this, in turn, will give you greater confidence in your caregiving role, whether you are a parent, grandparent or practitioner.

### Who am I?

At around the age of about 20 months, children become increasingly interested in the use of language. With the onset of language comes the sense of self as a separate individual with conscious opinions and desires. Adults very often lament the onset of the 'terrible twos', judging it to be one of the most trying and demanding phases of a child's life, because it is at this age that children begin to exert their will.

What has happened is that the small child has begun, in a very rudimentary way, to explore some of the most fundamental philosophical and spiritual questions: 'Who am I?' and 'What kind of person am I?'.

In order to learn about who we are and about the world around us, we need to feel safe and secure, within a loving and caring relationship. For two- to three-year-olds, it also means experiencing what it feels like to do the things that the grown-ups do. At this age, children are preoccupied with imitating or taking part in domestic life, whether it is dressing up in adult clothes, pretending to be asleep in a bed or helping to put dirty clothes into a washing machine.

## Domestic play

When children imitate domestic life, I describe it as being 'domestic play', which is a little different from imaginative play. Domestic play is the pretend or make-believe play with which the two-year-old is preoccupied. Domestic play is about copying the routine behaviours observed in adults, and this will change over time as our cultural behaviour changes. In the past ten years, even toddlers will put a mobile telephone to their ears and pretend to talk when, during the 1990s, it would have been an unfamiliar object to carry around or 'post'. Another preoccupation of the two-year-old is to play with familiar items from the home, such as kitchen equipment, cleaning utensils, clothes, bedding and objects from the bathroom. This is why the role-play area is such an important place in any nursery playroom.

In the 1980s, a local authority day nursery in West London went so far as to make the whole of the two- to three-year-olds' playroom into a role-play area to great success. It became 'like home', where the children had their afternoon naps and dressed up in the bedroom area, ate and were offered sensory play and painting in the kitchen area, looked at books and played with bricks, 'small world' toys and puzzles and so on in the living room area. While that arrangement may not suit most settings, it is worth considering whether or not the role-play area is big enough if you are working in a playroom with this age group.

### Pretending and make believe

When young children engage in domestic play, they are entering into a make-believe world. If you quietly observe a two- or three-year-old in the role-play area, you are likely to see him pretending to be a 'bossy mum', a 'crying baby' or the 'pet dog'. Objects may not be used as actual representations. A shampoo bottle might become a bottle of tomato ketchup, a wooden brick might become an iron and sand in a little pot might become a cup of tea.

This type of play is about pretending to be someone else and to 'feel' what that is like. Children will always be copying something they have

*Figure 8.1* Using objects from our real world enhances make-believe play and promotes language development

witnessed in their lives, whether it is at home, in another family home or at nursery. Indeed, the play of the two-year-old tends to be about ordinary domestic activity within family or nursery life.

The play is not just about activity; it is also about practising language. From the age of about 18 months there is a surge of language development. It is not surprising therefore that two-year-olds love to practise their newly found language skills and will often give a running commentary about what they are doing, whether someone is listening or not!

## Imaginative play

When we talk about imagination, we are referring to the ability to 'hold things in mind'. The *Collins English Dictionary* definition of the word 'imagination' is as follows:

- the faculty or action of producing mental images of what is not present or in one's experience;
- creative mental ability.

With the emergence of language, a box no longer serves as a container, as it did for the toddler engaged in Heuristic Play. A box now has the possibility of becoming a house, a car or a cupboard! It is the ability to give things a name that enables us to think in a reflective way.

Imaginative play goes much further than simply copying life's experiences, such as turning a box into a baby's cot. It is being able to create an image of something in your mind that is not there in front of you. While a two-year-old will tend to use the objects that are in front of them, a three- to five-year-old takes this much further and seeks out objects to 'turn into' magic creatures, potions, a space ship and so on. Indeed, the play of the over 3s can become very elaborate as one idea leads to another in their imaginations. This is where 'small world' material comes into its own, as children are able to imagine small cars or toy dinosaurs as being life-size and create 'vast worlds' of their own imaginings, even if they are only taking up a few square metres of the garden or playroom.

## Dens

All children, regardless of ages and culture, love to create dens. When I run my workshops and invite participants to recall their earliest memories of play, they invariably talk about the making of dens! At its most basic, a den might simply be a place that is under a table or in a cupboard. The finding, making and then playing in a den comes within the schema of 'enveloping', as all children have a fascination with wrapping and covering themselves up. This may start as hiding under a piece of cloth but, as children become more adventurous and imaginative, the den may take quite a long time to create and use various materials.

The appeal of a den also lies in the fact that children can be in a small (and often rather dark) place which is separate from the ordinary surroundings. Children can then play without being seen, yet they can often see out. There is something exciting and magical about being able to play out of sight, yet within reach, of others, particularly grown-ups. While children over three usually want to play in dens with others, the two- to three-year-olds often enjoy having the space for themselves and might spend quite a long time in their den. This is absolutely fine! You will need to help the younger children to create their den, but it is then important to leave them in peace once it is usable.

Here are some suggestions for basic material (for both inside and outside) to help the children get started:

*Figure 8.2* The role-play area allows the young child to copy routine and domestic behaviours observed in adults

- old sheets or blankets;
- large pieces of plastic sheeting (for outside);
- large boxes;
- a length of washing line or rope;
- parcel tape or strong clear tape;
- milk crates;
- small beach tent;
- wooden blocks;
- pieces of carpet or small rugs;
- cushions;
- a torch (for older children).

## The role-play area

The role-play area is probably the most important and most popular area in a typical playroom for the two- to three-year-olds. In recent years, the role-play area has been a space created with cupboards and dividers, with little doors and windows. It is usually filled with child-sized kitchen furniture, such as a cooker, sink and washing machine. Often, there will also be a dolly cot, table and chairs, together with some small plastic representations of objects we might find in a kitchen. This is often the place where children will find the dressing up clothes and shoes.

Some role-play areas have been equipped with very expensive furniture but have very little in the way of things to actually play with. Children of this age need plenty of 'real' objects rather than plastic toys and they also need additional furniture such as a child-sized bed or mattress with duvets and pillow so they can cover themselves up. It is also very important to have a large shatterproof mirror for the children to look at themselves. Many 'safe' mirrors are useless as they are either too small or they are more like sheets of stainless steel than a decent reflective mirror. Children need to be able to see their bodies clearly in full length.

When children are given 'real' representations of objects, whether they are small metal saucepans, or full-size mops and brooms (with cut-down handles) their play becomes more focused and sustained. In some settings, practitioners have even given children thick china crockery and have reported no breakages! Such play would, of course, have to be supervised, but children do seem to play much more carefully with real objects. However, you can buy very realistic crockery made out of plastic for the camping and barbecue market for the two-year-olds to use. Useful sources are kitchen shops, large supermarkets, camping shops, 'pound' shops and general household shops.

### Items for the role-play area

Here are some suggestions of items (in addition to the furniture already mentioned) that you might like to include in your role-play area (you may, of course, already have many of these but the possibilities are endless):

- dressing-up clothes with simple or no fastenings;
- shoes, hats and bags;
- dressing-up stand and hangers;
- large shatterproof mirror;
- child-sized ironing board and iron;
- small linen basket, bucket and empty bottle of clothes washing liquid;
- pegs and short length of washing line;
- tablecloth, place mats, coasters and napkins;
- artificial plant and flowers in a vase;
- tea towels, cleaning cloths, pan scrubs, washing up brushes and dusters;
- empty washing-up and polish bottles;
- full-sized metal pans and hooks for hanging them up;
- metal teapot and kettle;
- full-sized dishes, bowls, cups, tumblers, bread baskets and so on;
- set of real cutlery;

- wooden spoons and metal hand whisks;
- small tins and packets of food;
- pretend fruit and vegetables (wooden, plastic or homemade salt dough);
- real telephone and radio (unplugged and without batteries);
- empty shampoo, perfume and skin cream bottles;
- unbreakable hand mirrors, brushes and combs;
- hair accessories and jewellery;
- child–sized bed or mattress with pillows, cushions, sheets and duvet;
- dressed dolls;
- dolly cots with bedding and pillows (empty shoeboxes can be used).

## Links to the Early Years Foundation Stage (practice guidance)

### *Personal, Social and Emotional Development*

*Dispositions and attitudes*

- Explore the environment with interest.
- Discover more about what they like and dislike.
- Begin to develop self–confidence and a belief in themselves.

*Self-confidence and self-esteem*

- Feel pride in their own achievements.

*Making relationships*

- Learn social skills, and enjoy being with and talking to adults and other children.
- Seek out others to share experiences.
- Respond to the feelings and wishes of others.

*Behaviour and self-control*

- Begin to learn that some things are theirs, some things are shared and some things belong to other people.

### *Communication, Language and Literacy*

*Language for communication*

- Learn new words very rapidly and are able to use them in communicating about matters which interest them.

*Language for thinking*

- Use action, sometimes with limited talk, that is largely concerned with the 'here and now'.

### Problem Solving, Reasoning and Numeracy

*Numbers as labels and for counting*

- Use some number language, such as 'more' and 'a lot'.

Recognise groups with one, two or three objects.

*Calculating*

- Are learning to classify by organising and arranging toys with increasing intent.
- Begin to make comparisons between quantities.

### Knowledge and Understanding of the World

*Exploration and investigation*

- Use others as sources of learning and information.
- Explore, play and seek meaning in their experiences.

*Communities*

- Begin to have their own friends.

### Physical Development

*Using equipment and materials*

- Begin to make and manipulate objects and tools.
- Put together a sequence of actions.

### Creative Development

*Developing imagination and imaginative play*

- Pretend that one object represents another, especially when objects have characteristics in common.
- Begin to make-believe by pretending.

# CHAPTER 9

# Expanding the approach

## When language begins to develop

As children develop through their second year of life, their understanding of language begins to advance at a rapid rate. Alongside this growing ability to understand language is the driving impulse to communicate using words.

Up till now, a baby has used his voice to communicate his wants and needs through various noises, such as crying, gurgling, laughing, screaming and so on. However, there are also other ways that the baby communicates with others, such as facial expressions and the use of silence. Bodily movements, including level of rigidity, relaxation and reaching out to adults (including poking, tugging, caressing, etc.) all play their part in active communication as well.

When the ability to use words to communicate begins to develop during the second and third years of life, the whole world begins to take on new meaning and new possibilities. It is not the place of this book to examine language in detail. However, it is important to understand how the development of language changes the way in which children think in their play, particularly with reference to their use of objects in their play.

Offering household, recycled and natural objects as playthings to children who are developing the use of language opens up possibilities both for expressing creativity and initiative and for social interaction and negotiation.

## The Treasure Basket and the older child

Although the Treasure Basket has been developed specifically for the seated baby at the mouthing stage, the objects in the Basket will be of interest to all children. Indeed, it can sometimes be difficult to protect babies' Treasure Basket from the curious toddlers and older children wishing to select objects for their own play.

However, there can be a place for older children to really enjoy and gain much pleasure and learning from the Treasure Basket in their own right. If you already have a Treasure Basket for a group of babies, then it is probably a good idea to create a separate basket of objects for the older children. It is then always accessible, rather than having to borrow the babies' Treasure Basket.

## How old can the children be?

There is really no limit on the age at which a Treasure Basket can be of play value, but there are different ways in which you may want to use the resource for different age groups.

### 10–20 months (the toddler)

The Treasure Basket can be really useful when a toddler is tired or feeling in some way under the weather. It can be offered in a one-to-one situation with a trusted caregiver as a source of familiar comfort and interest. The adult needs to sit with the toddler and perhaps talk about the objects, offer them or generally interact more than with a seated baby. You will probably find that the toddler wants to put objects inside the purses, boxes, etc., bang things together, pick out similar objects and so on.

### 20 months to three years old

For this age group, the Treasure Basket can be used as an excellent stimulus for language. The adult, in this case, needs to sit with a small group of not more than three children and take the lead by naming objects and encouraging the children to do the same. The adult can also say what the functions of the objects are, what kind of noises they make, what the children are doing with the objects and so on. It is really important that the adult is responsive to the children wanting to 'show' what objects they have found because this is a very interactive and social way of using the contents of the basket.

### Three years and upwards

For this age group, there are various ways of using the Treasure Basket, depending on the level of the children's language ability and social skills:

- It can be used in the same way as for the 20-month to three-year-old age group.

- It can also be used to extend children's vocabulary, by not only naming the objects themselves, but also their characteristics, categories, functions, etc. and by encouraging the children to notice things like similarities and differences (such as in function, material, shape, etc.).

- A selected number of objects can be taken out to play 'Kim's Game', where the objects are put onto a tray and the children study them for a minute or two. A cloth is then used to cover the objects and the children have to see how many objects they can remember.

- A selected number of objects can be placed in a drawstring bag. The adult can put her hand inside, select an object and describe to the children to see if they can guess what the object is. This can be reversed so the child is doing the describing. Similarly, an object can be put in a bag (or several objects in several bags) and the children can feel and guess what the objects are without seeing them.

When children have reached the stage of being able to talk, the Treasure Basket can provide an excellent opportunity for language stimulation as well as being an enjoyable social activity with an adult and other children. However, it really needs to be used under the supervision of an adult and the objects should be kept with the basket, rather than being used as props for imaginative play. With initiative, plenty of other games for older children can be created with the Treasure Basket.

## Creating 'themed' Treasure Baskets

Another way in which the idea of the Treasure Basket can be developed for older children is to create several baskets with different themes. (These baskets would be in addition to a basic Treasure Basket, which has a mixture of everything.) Some themes might cover perishable items and so be only of short-term use. However, you may decide to create several different baskets, which could last for some time.

Some suggested themes (categorised by material) follow:

- wooden objects
- rubber objects
- metal objects
- glass objects
- leather objects
- fabric objects.

It is probably a good idea to avoid creating a basket of plastic objects as so many objects in the children's lives are now made of plastic.

Ideas for baskets categorised by function or location of objects are:

- bathroom objects
- kitchen objects
- pebbles and shells
- woodland objects
- things to wear
- different types of brushes
- jewellery
- boxes and purses
- large buttons
- various lids
- keys.

Baskets containing objects categorised by 'characteristic' might include:

- objects that have a scent
- empty bottles of perfume, shampoo, sun cream, hand cream, etc.
- objects that make a noise
- 'rough to touch' objects
- 'soft to touch' objects
- objects with handles
- objects that open and close
- objects characterised by colour
- pairs of matching objects (for example, two spoons, two shells, two sponges, etc.)
- transparent objects
- mirrors or other reflecting objects.

This is not a definitive list of themes, but rather a starting point of ideas from which you can develop your own themes, depending on your access to objects and your imagination.

## Heuristic Play and the older child

As children develop language they also become more sociable in that they seek out others to talk with and to share their ideas. Initially this interaction

*Figure 9.1* In the third year of life children begin to play together and use their imagination. Here a box and tubes have become a boat and mast

is with adults, but soon children from two years upwards want to 'tell' or 'show' their peers their ideas, activities and discoveries.

Although we all like to engage in solitary activity from time to time, human beings are social creatures and doing things with others brings activity to life and gives it more meaning and satisfaction. Even if a small child creates something on his own, it is very likely that he will seek out someone else to admire his creation!

## Playing with others

However, there is a very interesting shift from children playing alongside one another and copying what others are doing to using language (or other forms of communication such as gesture, etc.) to begin to share ideas and activities. It is the beginnings of 'let's do', 'let's make' and 'let's play', which form the basis of much of the play in childhood.

Despite the phenomenal increase in television viewing and computer use, children still say that what they like to do most is to play with their friends. A shared experience, whether it is a physical activity, creative enterprise, a game with rules or an imaginary game, is what enriches and delights children most.

### Heuristic Play as a way of life

It is both valuable and interesting to see how the principles of Heuristic Play and the open-ended materials that promote it can be offered to older children (from the age of two onwards). As the word 'heuristic' comes from the Greek word, 'eurisko', meaning 'I find', 'I discover', this kind of play could be seen as a way of life, rather than a stage of play in toddlerhood.

Open-ended play, which opens up the possibilities for self-discovery and increased awareness of oneself, provides the foundations for positive self-esteem, self-confidence, initiative, considered risk-taking and perseverance. When this type of play takes place with other children, then skills of negotiation, cooperation, leadership, sharing and empathy are also learned and developed.

With this in mind, the materials which are provided for Heuristic Play to toddlers can also successfully be offered to older children. They can use the materials and turn them into something else, whether it is food, clothing, weapons, vehicles or furniture. Sometimes, children like to use the materials to make something artistic and small scale, like a toy dinosaur enclosure or a castle. At other times, the material is used for life-sized props in an imaginary game (whether it is simple domestic play or within the realms of wild fantasy), such as using lids as plates or cardboard tubes as telescopes.

The most important thing is to allow the children to develop their own ideas, to talk to you about them and to respond appropriately to requests for support from the children. You may have to hold something physically in place while some fixing or sticking goes on, such as holding a box so that a child can slot a tube through a hole in its lid to make a funnel. You may be asked to help to repair something which has broken or fallen down, such as realigning a road made from parallel lines of bricks, which has accidentally been kicked. You will certainly need to provide plenty of material, to avoid conflict or disappointment.

In addition to the materials one can offer the toddler, you may wish to include further materials for older children, which have the possibility of either 'becoming something else' or 'holding materials together'. Some examples are:

- plenty of boxes of various sizes;

- sticky tape (particularly wide brown parcel tape);

- elastic bands;

- large and small sheets;

- dressing-up clothes;

- scissors, string and safety pins (under supervision);

- large tubes (insides of rolls of carpet);

- sheets of bubble wrap;

- silver foil (including milk bottle tops);

- planks of wood and sanded wood off-cuts;

- lengths of guttering, industrial tubing and drainpipe;

- plastic crates (from a dairy or supermarket);

- empty ice-cream tubs or other containers such as plastic flower pots;

- 'small world' figures, animals, trains, plans and cars.

So much of the play material or toys that are offered to children is manu-factured using sophisticated technology. However, many of these toys do not allow the children themselves to develop their own sophisticated thought. They have instant appeal, but are often quickly discarded because they do not stimulate individual creativity. It is often the very simple material which triggers the most sophisticated thinking and sustained play activity. The only way you will discover what the children will do and what more they might want is to present them with this kind of material and see what happens. Once again, the adult is best as an unobtrusive and attentive presence.

## How this approach can be used with children with special needs

It has already been described how the materials can be adapted for older children. However, the materials can also provide excellent play and learning opportunities for children with a learning difficulty or special need, because they can be enjoyed and appreciated regardless of a child's developmental stage.

Some children who have not yet developed language may have moved on from the toddler stage with regard to physical and self-help skills, but their play is still largely at the heuristic exploratory stage, rather than the imaginative stage.

Many children, who have learned to talk may, nevertheless, have not yet developed the Learning Tools (as described in Chapter 6) or may never have had the opportunity to handle a range of materials and still tend to put things in their mouths. Some children with a physical disability or sensory impairment, may have had limited experiences of handling a range of objects or experimenting with them.

### Diagnostic assessment

Over the past 28 years, as a practising educational psychologist, I have found that the Treasure Basket and Heuristic Play materials are invaluable tools for assessing the thinking and learning skills of young children.

When assessing a child with special needs, it is important to observe how he plays with the objects in a Treasure Basket or, separately, how he uses some collections of objects and containers for Heuristic Play.

Some useful questions to ask during an observation session with a Treasure Basket are:

- Does the child use all his senses when examining objects?
- Does the child examine the objects in detail or are the objects picked up and tossed away without exploration?
- How much mouthing is there?

For both the Treasure Basket and Heuristic Play objects and containers:

- Does the child show any anxiety about the objects or seek a high level of adult reassurance?
- Does the child show pleasure in these materials?
- How long is the child's interest sustained?
- Does the child initiate any interaction with the adult and, if so, how much?
- What evidence can you see that the child has developed the Learning Tools?
- Is the child using imagination with the materials as well as demonstrating Heuristic Play or mouthing?
- How much repetition is there in the play activity?

## *Ways in which the adult can use these materials to support the child with special needs*

- Many children with special needs require adult support, encouragement or even direction to help stimulate their play. Therefore, a child who has never automatically reached out, picked up and examined objects may need the adult to place an object from the Treasure Basket in his hand. The adult should sit very close to the child (either beside or in front) and at the same height so that there is a feeling of safety and togetherness in the experience.

- Similarly, some children may have missed out on the normal Heuristic Play stage and so would benefit greatly from the Heuristic Play objects and containers. Once again, the adult may have to intervene in the play in a more directed way, encouraging children to put bricks in containers, sorting out objects for similar characteristics, piling flat-sided objects on top of one another and so on.

- Another way in which the adult can support the child's play is to mimic what the child is doing and then develop the play further, so the child can then copy what the adult does next. It is important that the adult has an understanding of the Learning Tools and can actively teach them through 'doing' rather than just 'talking about' the concepts.

- The adult can also model appropriate play for the child who is showing no initiative with the materials, as a form of encouragement and stimulation.

# CHAPTER 10

# Conclusion

As the objects in the Treasure Basket and for Heuristic Play are open-ended, natural and household, there is a timeless quality about them. They will not date as they are not technologically or commercially fashionable. They do not require much expense and much of the material can be recycled when it is no longer required.

This material is inherently satisfying because it is varied and feeds the senses. Indeed, to play with these materials has an incredibly calming effect on babies, children and adults alike. There is something very grounding about simply messing about with ordinary things.

Although I have referred to it before, I feel that my final comment needs to relate to the use of plastic. While an immensely useful and versatile element in our lives, it has crept in and taken over the play of babies and young children. As most babies and young children spend the greater part of their lives away from nature, it becomes even more important that we introduce natural materials into their environment. Equally important is the need for caregivers to be attuned to the children and allow them to play at a natural pace.

# References and further reading

Ainsworth, M., Blehar, M., Waters, E. and Wall, S. (1978) *Patterns of Attachment: A Psychological Study of the Strange Situation*, Hillsdale, NJ: Lawrence Erlbaum.

Bettelheim, B. (1987) *A Good Enough Parent*, London: Thames & Hudson.

Bowlby, J. (1969) *Attachment*, London: Pelican.

Chugani, H., Behen, M., Muzik, O., Juhasz, C., Nagy, F. and Chugani, D. (2001) 'Local brain functional activity following early deprivation: a study of post-institutionalised Romanian orphans', *Neuroimage*, 14: 1290–1301, in Gerhardt, S. (2004), Hove: Brunner–Routledge.

Department for Education and Skills (DfES) (2007a) *Statutory Framework for the Early Years Foundation Stage*, Nottingham: DfES Publications.

Department for Education and Skills (DfES) (2007b) *Practice Guidance for the Early Years Foundation Stage*, Nottingham: DfES Publications.

Elfer, P., Goldschmied, E. and Selleck, D. (2003) *Key Persons in the Nursery: Building Relationships for Quality Provision*, London: David Fulton.

Gerhardt, S. (2004) *Why Love Matters*, Hove: Brunner–Routledge.

Goldschmied, E. and Hughes, A.M. (1992) *Heuristic Play with Objects* (film), London: National Children's Bureau. Reproduced in 2007 on DVD.

Goldschmied, E. and Jackson, S. (1994) *People Under Three: Young Children in Daycare*, London: Routledge.

Goldschmied, E. and Selleck, D. (1996) *Communication Between Babies in Their First Year*, London: National Children's Bureau (book and video).

Goleman, D. (1996) *Emotional Intelligence*, London: Bloomsbury.

Hughes, A.M. (1991) *I Don't Need Toys* (film), Suffolk: Concord Media. Reproduced in 2008 on DVD.

Hughes, A.M. (2009) *Problem Solving, Reasoning and Numeracy in the Early Years Foundation Stage*, London: Routledge.

Lieberman, A.F. (1995) *The Emotional Life of the Toddler*, New York: First Free Press.

Liedloff, J. (1986) *The Continuum Concept*, London: Arkana.

Stroh, K., Robinson, T. and Proctor, A. (2008) *Every Child Can Learn: Using Learning Tools and Play to Help Children With Developmental Delay*, London: Sage.

Winnicott, D.W. (1964) *The Child, the Family and the Outside World*, London: Pelican.

Winnicott, D.W. (1988) *Playing and Reality*, London: Pelican.